CANE · FILE BO[X]
FRAME · GYM
PAPER · NAME

· ASHTRAY · CLOCK · PURSE · JACKET · BLANKET
· KEYS · B[ ] · L [ ] T[ ] · NAILFILE
· SWEATER [ ]RT[ ]LE [ ]DIO PAPER CLIP
· DEODORAN[ ] SC[A]RF SHO[ ] · PERFUME
· EYEGLASS[ ] [ ]ND [ ] [ ]W[ ]D · THUMB-
TACKS · BRIEFCASE · KNUCKLES · DISHES
· ICE SCR[A]P[ ] · NECKLACE · WHISTLE ·
SEAT CUS[ ]NE MAGAZINE [ ]A[ ] MUSCLE
RUB · DECORATIONS · DENTAL FLOSS · OPEN
HAND · N[ ]T[ ]B[ ][ ]K [ ]A[ ][ ][ ][ ] HEAD ·
SUNGLASSES · PORTFOLIO · ANTENNA · HAT
· PUSH PIN · FOREARM · LIPSTICK BRUSH
· HAIRSPRAY · HEADBAND · SEAT BELT · FIN-
GERNAILS · TELEPHONE · PHOTOGRAPHS · STUN
GUN · EXERCISE MAT · DRINKING STRAW ·
BRACELET · LIGHTER · CURTAINROD · GLOVES
· VIDEO TAPE · HAIR CLIPS · HAIR · UMBRELLA
· METAL FAN · STAPLER · PHONE BOOK · KNEE
· LIGHT BULB · NAIL CLIPPERS · COINS · WRIST-
WATCH · CALENDAR · MIRROR · CASSETTE
TAPE · CALCULATOR · ELBOW · TALCUM POW-
DER · HAIRBRUSH · DRIVERS LICENSE · INKPEN
· HOUSEPLANT · ENVELOPE · LIGHT LENS ·
FOOT · CLIPBOARD · BROACH · UNDERGAR-
MENTS · TABLE · TWEEZERS · BARETTES ·
WHISK BROOM · SHIN · STOPWATCH · SHURIKEN
· COMPUTER DISKETTES · CREDIT CARDS ·
FILE FOLDERS · ARMLET · EYEBROW PENCIL
· CHAIR · COMB · BADGE · RINGS · PLAYING
CARDS · ANKLE WEIGHTS · RUBBER BANDS
· FOOTSTOOL · CURTAINS · KEYCHAIN KNIFE

101

WEAPONS

for Women

This book is dedicated to those women who have become unfortunate victims of abuse, assault, abduction, and rape. Hopefully, the research, development, and overall knowledge in this book will help prevent many of these crimes from occuring and will also relieve some of the anxiety and fear that so many women suffer because of them.

Rodney R. Rice

101
WEAPONS
for Women

IMPLEMENT WEAPONRY

Rodney R. Rice
Master Instructor

Published by
Ri-Jo PRODUCTIONS
Warrenton, VA

ACKNOWLEDGEMENTS

This book is the result of the imagination and creativity of martial artists who are concerned for women and their ability to effectively defend themselves. The author and publisher would like to thank the contributors for their time and energy given to the development of this much-needed concept of self defense.

The material in this book depicts an extremely controversial subject which is, "What should a woman *really* do to defend herself?" Many of these techniques may be considered deadly, some may even appear ridiculous, but the general opinion of the many people involved in this work has been very encouraging and optimistic regarding the subject. Without their approval, this book would not have been printed.

FIRST EDITION
101 Weapons for Women
Implement Weaponry
by Rodney R. Rice
edited by Lynn W. Jones
© 1991 by Ri-Jo Productions

Published by Ri-Jo Productions
P.O. Box 229, Warrenton, VA 22186
(703) 347-7266
**Call or write for additional books, video documentation,
and to schedule instructional seminars.**

Printed in the United States of America
ISBN: 0-9632402-1-8 10.95
Library of Congress Catalog Card Number: 92-93027

Some of the defensive techniques depicted in this book can cause serious injury. It is advised that great caution be taken in their practice and execution. The author and publisher hereby disclaim any and all responsibility or liability for injury that may occur as a result of the use or misuse of this material.

Table of Contents

Introduction

The attorney repeated himself. "Miss Evans, did you show any kind of resistance or give Mr. Johnson any *clear* reason to believe that you did not want to have sex with him?"

"Of course I did!" she responded hysterically. "I've known him for so long. I thought he was my friend. I never intended...."

She was interrupted by the attorney. "What resistance, specifically, did you offer?"

Self defense experts say that in the face of attack, a full 60% of victims would become paralyzed with fear; another 20% to 30% would fight back to no avail; and 10% to 20% would get away through physical self defense, verbal persuasion, or just plain luck. Besides fleeing, what is the most effective defense technique? Whether to scream, hit, run or comply—the decision is not an easy one.

Studies consistently show that women are three times more fearful of crime than men. The effects of this fear, of crime in general and sexual assault in particular, are pervasive and play a major role in where a woman chooses to work, where she lives, and what activities she elects to pursue.

Besides fleeing, what is the most effective defense technique?

Their fear is, in fact, well founded. According to the August 1989 issue of the Federal Bureau of Investigations *Uniform Crime Reports*, one forcible rape occurs every six minutes in the United States. This figure is probably underestimated, since many rapes go unreported. The records become even more chilling for aggravated assault, with an assault occurring every 35 seconds. Statistics show that one in three women will be assaulted during her lifetime. Over half of the reported assaults on women take place in their own homes; eighty percent are committed by an unarmed assailant.

In a study involving nearly one hundred women

who either were raped or who avoided rape in an assault situation, researchers Pauline Bart and Patricia O'Brien found that besides fleeing, the most effective way to avoid assault is to respond with many different defensive techniques, such as screaming and physical force. Pleading and crying were found to be ineffective defensive strategies.

They also determined that the sooner a woman defends herself, the more likely she is to avoid rape. While women who resisted their attackers were more likely to suffer minor injuries such as scrapes and bruises, they were no more likely to suffer serious injury than those women who did not resist.

Emotional injury is an equally important factor in the perceived benefit of resisting an assault. It is common for an assault victim to report in counseling that she feels in some way that she is a bad or tainted person. Victims often tell their counselors they feel somehow responsible for what has happened. Another common feeling among female assault victims is that they should have done something different, or they did not do all they could or should have done in order to deter the attack.

The more immediately a woman defends herself, the more likely she is to avoid rape.

All the experts seem to agree on one thing: a woman needs to be prepared for the worst. This may be easier said than done. In this present world of modern conveniences, many of us are just not ready for physical violence, and would be caught so totally off guard we might be frozen by our fear. Some women may feel squeamish or uneasy while reading parts of this book because it depicts violent acts for one's defense.

Interestingly enough, women frequently believe that they would have little problem reacting with physical violence toward an attacker if he were threatening their children. Although their maternal instincts permit them to visualize seriously injuring an attacker in defense of their children, even to the point of death, women admit they cannot conceive defending themselves to the same degree when their own lives are being threatened.

The U.S. Constitution provides the right for us to bear arms. American founding fathers saw the necessity for us to defend ourselves from the hostile world. We have the right to fight back. By gaining knowledge and accumulating defensive options, a woman increases her choices in an attack situation. Based even on the range of personalities among women, some of the techniques in *101 Weapons for Women* will feel more comfortable to some women than others. Certainly some defenses are more appropriate than others in specific situations.

Despite a woman's best effort, she never knows when she may be the potential victim of attack. Being familiar with the information contained in *101 Weapons for Women* will greatly increase her chances of preventing and/or surviving an assault. All women desiring greater confidence in their ability to successfully defend themselves against an attack should read and study this book.

Are You a Target?

Take this quiz to determine if you might be a vulnerable target.

Consider each question carefully and answer yourself as honestly as possible. Turn to page 110 for scoring and for Parts II and III of your Personal Safety Profile.

1. Which one statement best describes your dress code:
A. I prefer a more classic or traditional image.
B. I like to be comfortable with room to move.
C. I look better in clothes which show my figure.

2. As you walk, do you:
A. carry yourself with confidence? Yes/No
B. daydream or stare at the ground? Yes/No
C. move with a quick, strong gait? Yes/No
D. swing your purse or belongings? Yes/No
E. look ahead and to the sides for potential trouble? Yes/No

3. Which pair of traits is most a part of your personality?
A. alert and assertive
B. agreeable and cooperative
C. passive and obedient

4. Do your physical qualities include any of the following?
A. small in size   B. weak or frail   C. handicapped

5. How would you react to...
A. Someone looking you in the eyes:
      1. return their gaze   2. blush or look away
B. Being served cold or badly prepared food in a restaurant:
      1. send it back   2. keep it
C. Having a peer speak falsely about you to your boss or teacher:
      1. let the incident pass   2. defend your reputation

6. Do you become fearful if:
A. someone gives you a mean look? Yes/No
B. you are home alone and hear strange noises? Yes/No
C. the phone rings but no one responds or the caller hangs up? Yes/No
D. someone raises his or her voice at you? Yes/No

7. Which way do you respond when frightened?

A. become confused and disoriented

B. feel weak or paralyzed   C. react with emotion

D. react with violence   E. rapidly gain control of myself

8. How many things do you consciously do to avoid being a victim of crime? *(for example, locking doors and windows)*

Total:_____

9. Do you agree or disagree with each statement?

A. My home or office is in a high-crime area. Agree/Disagree

B. I feel uncomfortable working around some co-workers. Agree/Disagree

C. I always obey my instincts about safety. Agree/Disagree

D. I don't allow people to put me in compromising positions. Agree/Disagree

E. My boyfriend respects my attitudes and moral choices. Agree/Disagree

10. Which sums up your attitude about crime?

A. I am aware of potential dangers and hazards.

B. I am confident that I will not be victimized.

C. I try not to think about crime.

11. How do you use alcohol (or drugs)?

A. not at all   B. 1-2 drinks, once or twice a week

C. 1-2 drinks daily   D. usually 3 or more drinks at a time

E. 3 or more drinks, three or more times a week

12. You would say about your schedule and travel:

A. I am spontaneous; every day is different.

B. I am efficient and have a set routine.

C. I have a basic framework I like to stick to, but usually have lots of errands.

13. Do you carry valuables that others would know about?

Yes/No

14. Finally—do you know for sure that you could and would fight back if you had to?

Yes/No

CANE · FILE BOX · PENCIL · PILLOW · PICTURE
FRAME · GYM BAG · FLOOR MATS · NEWS-
PAPER · NAMETAG · MACE · WRIST · BELT
· ASHTRAY · CLOCK · PURSE · JACKET · BLANKET
· KEYS · B _ · L _ TO _ · NAILFILE
· SWEATER · _RT _LE _ADIO _ PAPER CLIP
· DEODORAN_ _ S__F SHO_ · PERFUME
· EYEGLASS__ __ND __OW__D · THUMB-
TACKS · BRIEFCASE · KNUCKLES · DISHES
· ICE SCRA_ER · NECKLA_E · WHISTLE ·
SEAT CUS___ ___MAGAZI__ ___A_· MUSCLE
RUB · DECO_ATIONS · DENTAL FLOSS · OPEN
HAND · N__B__K · _AR___N_T · HEAD ·
SUNGLASS__ · PORTFOLIO · ANTENNA · HAT
· PUSH PIN · FOREARM · LIPSTICK BRUSH
· HAIRSPRAY · HEADBAND · SEAT BELT · FIN-
GERNAILS · TELEPHONE · PHOTOGRAPHS · STUN
GUN · EXERCISE MAT · DRINKING STRAW ·
BRACELET · LIGHTER · CURTAINROD · GLOVES
· VIDEO TAPE · HAIR CLIPS · HAIR · UMBRELLA
· METAL FAN · STAPLER · PHONE BOOK · KNEE
· LIGHT BULB · NAIL CLIPPERS · COINS · WRIST-
WATCH · CALENDAR · MIRROR · CASSETTE
TAPE · CALCULATOR · ELBOW · TALCUM POW-
DER · HAIRBRUSH · DRIVERS LICENSE · INKPEN
· HOUSEPLANT · ENVELOPE · LIGHT LENS ·
FOOT · CLIPBOARD · BROACH · UNDERGAR-
MENTS · TABLE · TWEEZERS · BARETTES ·
WHISK BROOM · SHIN · STOPWATCH · SHURIKEN
· COMPUTER DISKETTES · CREDIT CARDS ·
FILE FOLDERS · ARMLET · EYEBROW PENCIL
· CHAIR · COMB · BADGE · RINGS · PLAYING
CARDS · ANKLE WEIGHTS · RUBBER BANDS
· FOOTSTOOL · CURTAINS · KEYCHAIN KNIFE

101 WEAPONS for Women

Be in Control

Even though it was early May, Ruth's suntan was just starting to turn a lush, golden brown. After church one Sunday, she had nothing better to do than change into her swimsuit, oil down, and toast in the afternoon Texas sunshine. The pool area was just starting to get a little crowded. To avoid the rapidly rising noise level, she settled into a vacant corner spot and diverted her attention to the novel she was reading.

The peace and quiet didn't last long, however. A party of noisemakers had made their way to Ruth's end of the pool. Trying to ignore them, she continued to appear deeply absorbed in her book. As the revelry drew closer, it became impossible for her to read and enjoy roasting in the sun. Ruth gathered her belongings and prepared to leave.

As she rose from the lounge chair and reached for her beach robe, a burly man grabbed hold of her, picked her up, and threw her into the pool. Ruth sputtered to the surface, adjusting her suit to make a decent emergence from the water. She quickly made her way back to collect her items, only to have the same brute repeat his performance. Hitting the water on her back, she felt a flash of pain along with her fear and anger. She made for the nearest ladder and climbed out, her new-found friend awaiting another opportunity to play his game.

She had no intention of returning to the pool nor allowing his agression to harm her.

This time, Ruth was ready for him. As he grabbed for her, she had no intention of returning to the pool nor allowing his agression to harm her. She reacted in the best way she could at the time by stabbing with her thumbnail into the base of his throat. To her surprise (and his!), blood spurted out. His friends came to his rescue, allowing Ruth to leave amid the confusion. Ruth later learned that her pool-side assailant had to be transported to the emergency room for medical attention. She also learned that she could protect herself with a long thumbnail. She was never again bothered at the pool.

Do not let yourself become a submissive victim unnecessarily. If you are physically threatened or your life is at risk, it is not impractical to defend yourself by whatever means possible. Many victims later feel responsible for an attack or crime—if only they could have done something to prevent it, or at least shown some kind of resistance. Remember that many times an attack can be minimized or completely avoided by simply fighting back, either verbally or physically.

This argument is not meant to instill a false sense of confidence by saying that *any* assault can be prevented by this approach to self defense. There are certain situations when resisting could complicate matters or cost the victim's life, such as when the attacker cannot be effectively stopped or an escape cannot be made. There have been many cases of abuse and rape in which a woman cooperated with the attacker knowing it would save her life, but there are also cases in which her cooperation failed to save her.

Learn how common crimes occur, and plan ahead to remove as much risk as you possibly can.

Only you can determine what you should do at that time, if and when it becomes necessary. If you make the decision not to submit to being victimized, it must be a positive choice to be effective. In this book are methods to apply in your positive decision to defend yourself.

Your first line of defense begins long before a confrontation takes place. Learn how common crimes occur, and plan ahead to remove as much risk as you possibly can.

Planning ahead includes getting to know neighbors and keeping an eye out for each other; leaving lights on when you will be returning after dark; replacing locks at a new residence and keeping doors, windows, and cars locked at all times; and keeping shades pulled after dark. Keep your car in good repair with a full gas tank. Take time to move your car closer to your office when you know you will be working late, and have your car keys ready in advance.

Remember that there is safety in numbers. Travel or leave a place with a friend whenever possible. Stay in well-lit, busy places. Avoid stepping into an elevator, automobile, or other confined area with a stranger. Don't allow a stranger to enter your home— a legitimate sales or repair person will allow you to verify employment with their office.

Your personal attitude and conduct can also make you a less likely target for crime. For safety at home, use only your last name and initial on doors, mail-boxes, and in the phone book. Never leave a note on the door saying when you will return or where to pick up house keys. Use a peephole to be certain of a caller's identity before opening the door, even if you have a chain lock.

Away from home, carry yourself alertly and with confidence; don't look like easy prey. Flashy clothing and flashing money or jewelry invite attack. Dress conservatively, for freedom of movement, and hold valuables firmly against your body. Keep purchases and other items in your car hidden in the trunk or under the seat.

Your personal attitude and conduct can also make you a less likely target for crime.

Never admit an unknown passenger into your car. If you feel you are being followed while driving, do not lead them to your home; instead, go to the police station or an open store or business and immediately report the incident. Try to give the license number and description of the vehicle. If your car should break down, raise the hood, tie a white "flag" to the antenna, and remain in the car with the doors locked. When someone offers help, keep the window high enough to prevent any entry and ask them to report the trouble to the nearest service station. Though it may be unsafe to accept or offer a ride, you can report others' car trouble as well.

Your best defenses are your senses. Always be looking ahead for alleys, groups of people, dead-ends —any potentially unsafe conditions. Check to the sides of doorways and in the back seat of your car. Listen for approaching footsteps.

Most of all, trust your instincts. If you don't feel safe, you probably shouldn't be there. Don't be afraid to ask for help or call the police; your own safety and well-being are far too important.

DATE RAPE

Date rape occurs largely due to our social training: women are often taught to be submissive and compliant, while surveys show that men (and women) believe such things as when women say no they actually mean yes, or that it is o.k. to force a woman to have sex if the man spent a lot of money on a date or was "led on." Date rape often occurs in someone's home or automobile. It is growing more common among college and high school campuses and dormitories. Though a woman should never feel guilty or ashamed of being victimized, there are precautions she herself can take to reduce the likelihood of such an incident.

Surveys show that men (and women) believe such things as when women say no they actually mean yes.

Don't imagine that just because you have a date with this man, he would never hurt or rape you. Get to know that person very well by going on group dates. Even with someone you feel you know, stick to dinner and a movie rather than "parking" or being alone in an apartment. Avoid alcohol or other substances that impair judgement, and remember that if your date is drinking, his perception of you may be inaccurate. Be aware of signals you are giving off; don't expect him to believe your "No" when your body language says "Yes." Because your date is someone you know, consider telling him as a deterrent that you will definitely press charges .

ABUSE IN THE HOME

If you are one of the many battered wives in the United States, you already know that spouse abuse is a cycle. The only way to break it is to make a positive decision that you cannot and will not continue to be a victim in your home. Report the abuse to family, the police, social services, or family counseling.

In the event that the abuser will not agree to counseling or you are not willing to take such steps, there are other avenues that may provide relief. Joining a support group will preserve your self-esteem and help you not become co-dependent. Analyze the pattern of the abuse—is it on weekends involving alcohol, does it build for six or eight weeks at a time, do you find yourself repeating arguments and walking into the same trap—and see if you can defuse the situation. Realize also that as the victim, the abusive pattern will likely be beyond your control. When all else fails, go with your children to a safe place for the evening.

ROBBERY

If you are the victim of robbery, remember that your safety is irreplaceable. Calmly comply with requests for items and money. To increase chances of recovery, though, there are several points to bear in mind. First, you can stall for time for someone to notice your plight.

Gather a description of the robber and report it to the police immediately.

Without being obvious, gather a description of the robber and report it to the police immediately. As you stall, consider what your reaction might be if the robber should threaten you physically.

Learn how to make every effort possible to be in control of threatening situations you might find yourself in. In the event of an attempted crime against you or an actual physical confrontation, be determined that you will consciously influence the outcome.

Attack Situation Chart

This chart illustrates a range of emotions an assailant and victim might experience, their intentions in an attack situation, and methods to carry out those intentions.

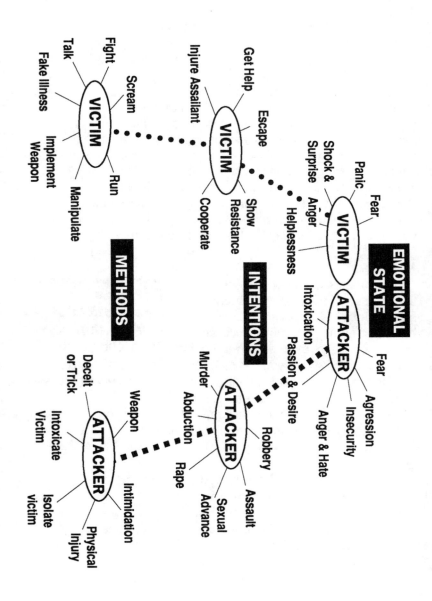

Implement Weaponry

Martial arts instructors and law enforcement officers alike are constantly bombarded with inquiries by women concerned with self defense, especially when there has been a vicious crime involving a woman. The subject of women's self defense is a growing concern in this country.

Most women ask the same thing: "Is there a quick, short-cut version of self defense I can learn, at an inexpensive cost?" To most women's disappointment, they are advised that the best way to become proficient in their ability to confidently defend themselves against an attacker is to train hard and long in a quality self defense program.

Over the years, a compassion has been developed for these women and their tremendous fear and insecurity, as they seek protection from the multitudes of physical crimes committed against them. There is no one, magical technique that will always prevent every assailant from performing his agressive act, but the use of Implement Weaponry can provide an effective approach to women's self defense.

A great majority of women become helpless victims unnecessarily, because of their lack of confidence. A woman's immediate reaction to an attack situation can determine whether or not she is easy prey for an assailant to carry out his intentions. Do not underestimate the extreme psychological effect your initial reaction will have—potential assailants will often be deterred if proper resistance or forceful refusal can be demonstrated. Many women are victims of repeated abuse simply because they are never able to fight back or make the abuse known to those who can help them. Proper mental attitude and response to an attack situation is imperative in effectively evading assault.

Aside from your physical capabilities, two major

> *There is no one, magical technique that will always prevent every assailant from performing his agressive act.*

factors in defending yourself adequately are, first, your *will* to help yourself against an attacker, and second, how you *present* your decision not to become a submissive victim. Even training to become a black belt in the martial arts would be of little use without developing the will and the confidence to use what you have learned if it became necessary.

Authorities in emergency medicine and rescue work attempt to keep victims calm and in control of their wits. Panic and fear are the worst enemies to self-help and survival, as they are usually accompanied by total loss of control. The results can range from extreme physical weakness, such as fainting or paralysis, to overpowering surges of adrenalin and strength. Martial arts training is definitely one way of developing the mental skill to control yourself, and though it is strongly recommended, very few women possess the time or dedication required to obtain such skill.

One purpose of this book is to give women a direct and practical approach to protecting themselves without being trained in the martial arts, by incorporating the many Implement Weapons available at their immediate disposal. This book does *not* address the multitude of situations one might find oneself in, but illustrates Implement Weapons applied to vital target areas without limiting their use with step-by-step procedures. Another goal of this book is to help make women aware that anywhere, anytime, almost anything can be used to give them an offensive advantage in deterring a potential assailant.

> **Training to become a black belt would be of little use without the will and confidence to use what you have learned.**

The thought and focus used to apply the weapon can not only elevate your state of mind by making you more alert and confident, but could also intimidate an assailant. Most women are afraid to use their hands against an attacker. Given an extension of their hands by incorporating a nearby Implement Weapon, they can become mentally better capable of self defense.

This book contains the most effective or deadly weapons closest to women at all times, regardless of where they might be or whatever the situation. Keep in mind that this book is intended to stimulate thought, awareness, and common sense, and the idea that there may always be an alternative to becoming totally submissive, such as the use of a weapon in self defense.

The items in this book have been researched and selected very carefully. The applications should be considered very seriously and are by no means limited or restricted to those depicted.

If you consider the ancient martial arts that involve weaponry, you will find that most of them evolved around simple farm implements, household items, clothing, and personal wares. The use of many of these items was rehearsed and developed into effective art forms of killing or warding off enemies.

This book contains ten general categories of the most common items that may be implemented as weapons. The application of the items to the attacker's vital spots is described in very short and direct terms. The proper use of many of the items requires quick and forceful execution. If you have the opportunity to resist becoming the victim of an attack and you have determined resistence is appropriate, a *positive* commitment to an evasive tactic must be made in order to successfully allow you to escape, or to prevent or disable your assailant from continuing.

This book contains the most immediate and practical items that may become effective or deadly weapons.

There is nothing complicated about the application of Implement Weapons. It only requires a little common sense and a determination to fight back. Please note that many of these techniques can cause serious injury and even death.

Do not misunderstand that there are situations when resisting an assault can endanger your life. Know that weapons of any sort may be taken away and used against you—even police officers have been killed by their own guns. The decision whether or not to fight back is one you must make for yourself depending on the circumstances.

Awareness and confidence are the key ingredients in effectively utilizing the knowledge in this handbook. One of the best ways to achieve this is to study the photographs over and over again, memorizing the applications of each weapon. Another method of using this handbook is to actually rehearse the techniques with a partner, creating different situations from various positions. Use your imagination and creativity on how these principles might apply to a situation you could find yourself in. Please use extreme caution not to injure your partner while practicing.

Keep this handbook with you at all times: in your purse, car, or pocket as a constant reminder of what it contains. By carrying it with you as a reference, you will feel more confident about your ability to take care of yourself. Make it a daily point to be more aware of the list of items in your handbook, even memorizing all 101 of them! You might even want to keep many of these items with you or go out and purchase some of them for added security.

Despite planning and precautions, any woman may find herself a potential victim of attack. What she does then could determine the outcome of the incident. Here are six steps to remember and follow should you be placed in such a situation.

If you are a Victim

1...DO NOT PANIC OR SHOW FEAR

A potential assailant is looking for an easy victim. Remember, your level of confidence and state of mind is directly reflected in the way you physically present yourself. Your posture, voice, eyes, and body movement in general can be extremely important factors in hindering a potential attacker. The appearance of strength is a good psychological weapon against an assailant.

2...MAKE A DECISION TO DEFEND YOURSELF

Quickly and carefully evaluate your situation. Depending on the circumstances, make a *positive* decision that you are not going to become a submissive victim of attack or abuse. Do not make this decision half-heartedly by letting your mind bounce back and forth about whether you can handle yourself or not. A positive commitment must be made to fight back in order to defend yourself effectively.

3...IDENTIFY YOUR WEAPON

One thing that will immediately help your state of mind is to quickly identify the most practical item near you that could apply as a weapon. Knowing the items on you and around you that are listed in this handbook should give you the confidence to better help yourself and stay calm.

4...IDENTIFY THE VITAL TARGET

Look at the potential assailant with total intent of inflicting the necessary injury to deter or disable him from going any further. According to his physical stature, you would want to find the most accessible vital spot (see *Vital Points Chart*). Additionally, it may be necessary to manipulate the attacker into the most advantageous position for effectively using your weapon and inflicting injury.

5...MOMENT OF OPPORTUNITY

The most effective timing in the execution of your defensive technique will usually, but not always, be to respond immediately. The key factor in properly defending yourself is to catch your attacker off guard. Shock or surprise him. If an immediate reaction will not accomplish this, cooperating until you can achieve surprise may become necessary.

6...EXECUTE THE TECHNIQUE EFFECTIVELY

Once you have selected a weapon and identified a vital target area, and the timing is appropriate, you must apply the technique with enough seriousness and force to be effective to the point of escaping the situation, deterring the attack, or even inflicting critical or non-recuperative injury upon the assailant. A strong verbal reaction, such as yelling or screaming, will increase the effect of your technique.

Vital Points of Attack

The human body is very easily injured. Think about it: the slightest fall could break your neck or back; a minor bump can cause serious internal damage; even a small cut might result in bleeding to death. The human body is actually one of the most frail of all creatures on earth. Though our minds can be trained to tolerate incredible pain, the slightest scratch or wound is very discomforting and painful. In other words, to inflict a distracting or even serious injury on someone is not too difficult to achieve in self defense.

The vital points shown here are the most vulnerable targets at which to apply your Implement Weapon, though the severity of each attack can range from causing discomfort, to a painful injury needing first aid, to a major injury requiring medical attention. If one's life or moral integrity is threatened by an assailant, it would not be unreasonable to inflict a bleeding or non-recuperative wound. Any other area not indicated is not considered a practical or realistic target for the use of Implement Weapons.

DEGREE OF SEVERITY

Each photograph of Implement Weapon applications depicts either first, second, or third degree injury inflicted on the assailant. The degree of injury depends both on the method of application and on the vital area targeted. This does not imply that a single weapon nor a given target will always result in the same degree of injury.

1– Discomfort and distraction
2– Pain and minor injury
3–Injury requiring medical attention

An attacker may be identified or traced by items collected at the scene: clothing fibers, blood and skin cells, strands of hair, etc.; and by a visit to the emergency room or physician. Any marks or injuries on an attacker could also help to identify and convict him.

Vital Points Chart

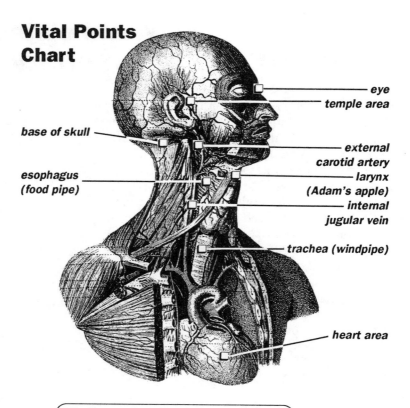

eye

temple area

base of skull

external
carotid artery

esophagus
(food pipe)

larynx
(Adam's apple)

internal
jugular vein

trachea (windpipe)

heart area

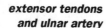

The human body is very easily injured.

extensor tendons
and ulnar artery

muscle attachments,
radial and ulnar arteries & veins

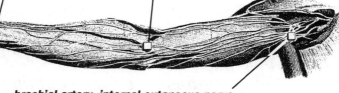

brachial artery, internal cutaneous nerve,
musculo-spiral nerve

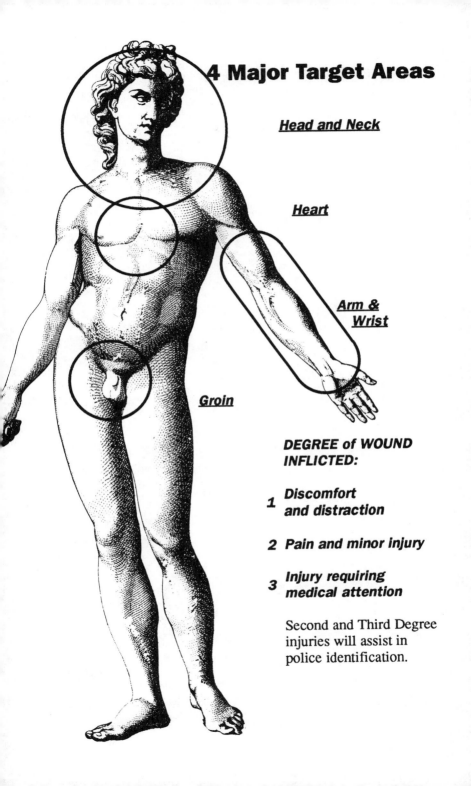

4 Major Target Areas

**Head and Neck**

**Heart**

_**Arm &
Wrist**_

**Groin**

**DEGREE of WOUND
INFLICTED:**

**1 Discomfort
and distraction**

2 Pain and minor injury

**3 Injury requiring
medical attention**

Second and Third Degree
injuries will assist in
police identification.

Anything is a weapon...

I was preparing a self defense presentation for a women's group, along with my tae kwon do master instructor. We decided to show the application of some items which anyone could use to injure an attacker. He picked up a magazine and before I could react, he quickly brushed the edge of the pages across my face, leaving three bleeding cuts at the corner of my eye.

I was shocked and for a moment disoriented. I couldn't believe the accuracy and effect of what he had just done to my face with that magazine. I'll never forget what he said to me as the blood was trickling down the side of my cheek: "Anything is a weapon."

From that moment I was inspired to research and develop the concept of Implement Weapons.

I'm sure we have all seen the classic barroom brawl in the movies where they fight it out with chairs, pictures, and bottles; and the James Bond scenes where he pulls his fancy gadgets out of an ink pen or briefcase and kills the enemy; or the angry housewife throwing plates and other dishes through the air at her husband in an outrage. Then there is always the pie in the face or the drink in the eyes routine.

Before I could react, he quickly brushed the edge of the pages across my face.

Remember that an assailant isn't looking for a fight–he's looking for a victim. By showing resistance to your attacker by using the items near you, he can become shocked, confused, and disoriented to the point of changing his mind entirely, or hesitating long enough for you to escape or turn the circumstances around. Some of the techniques and weapons depicted in this book can obviously cause critical injury.

The weapons around you are innumerable and may be applied in a multitude of variations. Thorough study of this handbook should give you the insight to be more aware and creative in just what you could do to defend yourself using anything as a weapon.

IMPORTANT

A strong verbal reaction must accompany your defensive techniques in order to maximize their effectiveness. Firm commands and protests, screaming, and threats of prosecution have proven to be successful deterrents against male aggression. In martial arts training, yelling is practiced to develop speed, power, and confidence, and to intimidate the opponent. In addition, verbally expressing your resistance to the attacker will reinforce your decision and could give you better control in a situation.

CANE · FILE BOX · PENCIL · PILLOW · PICTURE
FRAME · GYM BAG · FLOOR MATS · NEWS-
PAPER · NAMETAG · MACE · WRIST · BELT
· ASHTRAY · CLOCK · PURSE · JACKET · BLANKET
· KEYS · _____ · _____ · _____ · NAILFILE
· SWEATER _____ · PAPER CLIP
· DEODORAN_____ SC_RF SHO_ · PERFUME
· EYEGLASS_____ ND_____ D · THUMB-
TACKS · BRIEFCASE · KNUCKLES · DISHES
· ICE SCRAPER · NECKLACE · WHISTLE ·
SEAT CUS_____ · MUSCLE
RUB · DECO_ATIONS · DENTAL FLOSS · OPEN
HAND · N_____ HEAD ·
SUNGLASS_S · PORTFOLIO · ANTENNA · HAT
· PUSH PIN · FOREARM · LIPSTICK BRUSH
· HAIRSPRAY · HEADBAND · SEAT BELT · FIN-
GERNAILS · TELEPHONE · PHOTOGRAPHS · STUN
GUN · EXERCISE MAT · DRINKING STRAW ·
BRACELET · LIGHTER · CURTAINROD · GLOVES
· VIDEO TAPE · HAIR CLIPS · HAIR · UMBRELLA
· METAL FAN · STAPLER · PHONE BOOK · KNEE
· LIGHT BULB · NAIL CLIPPERS · COINS · WRIST-
WATCH · CALENDAR · MIRROR · CASSETTE
TAPE · CALCULATOR · ELBOW · TALCUM POW-
DER · HAIRBRUSH · DRIVERS LICENSE · INKPEN
· HOUSEPLANT · ENVELOPE · LIGHT LENS ·
FOOT · CLIPBOARD · BROACH · UNDERGAR-
MENTS · TABLE · TWEEZERS · BARETTES ·
WHISK BROOM · SHIN · STOPWATCH · SHURIKEN
· COMPUTER DISKETTES · CREDIT CARDS ·
FILE FOLDERS · ARMLET · EYEBROW PENCIL
· CHAIR · COMB · BADGE · RINGS · PLAYING
CARDS · ANKLE WEIGHTS · RUBBER BANDS
· FOOTSTOOL · CURTAINS · KEYCHAIN KNIFE

101 WEAPONS for Women

Clothing

It's no news that everyone wears clothes. The things you wear probably have the widest variety of application of any of the Implement Weapons. You may even locate weapons of self defense among the clothing your assailant is wearing; for example, choking him with his own tie.

One method of using your clothing for self defense would be not necessarily to inflict injury, but to show resistance in order to escape or deter the attack. Other items, such as hard shoe or boot heels, belt buckles, eyeglasses and hair accessories may be used to cause injury when applied by striking the assailant.

Remember the timing that is necessary to arrive at the "moment of opportunity" (see *If you are a Victim*). The removal of clothing in order to use it in self defense may require a strategy or manipulation. Stay calm and do not arouse suspicion as you maneuver. Then, when you are ready, use speed of execution to make your technique more shocking and more effective.

Firmly grasp a short portion of the scarf and push away, across assailant's eyes.

Clothing
...Scarf

Accessories such as scarves and shawls are usually easily removed and may be suddenly thrown around an attacker's neck and twisted or pulled. They can also be used to push an attacker away by his neck or eyes. Covering his face and eyes will confuse him and may increase the effectiveness of additional defensive techniques.

Scarves are often made of silk or other fine materials and therefore may be used almost like a rope for grappling or tying an attacker's hands or entangling his feet.

Twisting and circling scarf around neck.

1– Discomfort and distraction
2– Pain and minor injury
3– Injury requiring medical attention

Throwing shawl over back of neck and pulling down.

Clothing
...Shoes

There are many different types of shoes. Whether heels, boots, or tennis shoes, all can make good weapons. The most practical application, of course, is to kick or stomp the attacker. A sudden kick, even to the shin, could prove effective.

You might find yourself in a situation where you have removed your shoes, perhaps in order to use them as a weapon. Remember to identify any shoe that might be available as a potential weapon for self-defense. Shoe laces and speed-lace grommets may be applied in ways shown in other sections of this book.

Even if you have fallen or been pushed down, you can attack to groin or face.

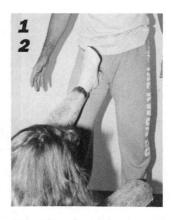

Shoes placed on hands, thrust to throat.

Shoe heels can be lifted or pulled upward into the groin.

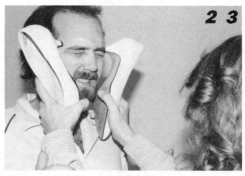

Attack with a hammer motion, then rake heels across temples.

Clothing
...Eyeglasses

Two hands thrusting
hard temple of glasses
into the throat.

Glasses can become excellant weapons for several reasons. They are among the most common and accessible items to use in self defense. Sunglasses are popular year-round, especially at vacation spots where many women may be targeted for crime. An attack with glasses will likely shock the assailant.

Made of metal, glass, or plastic, the hard and sharp edges easily penetrate the skin. Raking or pulling the temple edge across the skin can cut like a knife, leaving serious injury. The ear-pieces may be used to poke the eyes or gouge into the neck or groin.

Stabbing into the eyes.

Long, thin earpiece is
easily poked into the
eyes.

Clothing
...Purse

Prevention first: never carry your purse by the strap over your shoulder in a suspicious area or situation. An attacker can use it to pull you or drag you down.

An assailant will not expect to be hit with a purse, nor with many of the other Implement Weapons. The weight of a heavy purse can injure a person easily, especially if contact is made with a metal buckle or clasp. You will maintain better balance and control if you hold the purse itself rather than swinging it by the strap. Beating an attacker back and forth can be most effective.

Whipping the purse back and forth across the face.

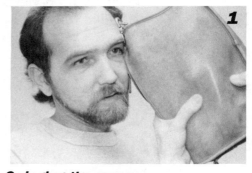

Swinging the purse sideways to the temple.

Swinging the purse upward to the groin.

A sudden thrust or push into the attacker's neck.

Clothing
...Belt

Detering the attack by wrapping and twisting the belt around the neck.

Belt buckle prong pressed into throat.

The leather strap is a universal item. It has been used for virtually everything, from harnessing a horse to holding up one's pants. In fact, the attacker probably wears a belt which you could obtain for self defense.

Metal buckles and prongs become effective weapons when swung at an attacker or pushed into his throat.

The belt itself can be wrapped around the neck and used to pull the attacker straight to the ground. It can also be used to secure the assailant's feet or hands to prevent pursuit or further attack.

Sling buckle-end of belt into face or temple to strike, injure, and disorient assailant.

Clothing
...Coat

As coats, sweaters, and even heavy sweatshirts are removed, they can become attack deterrents. It may sound silly, but picture pulling your sweater over an attacker's head in order to escape. Once he is trapped and blindfolded by your sweater or coat, you can drag him in circles to make him dizzy until he falls down.

Flinging your coat against the side of his face will distract the assailant and show resistance. Leather coats or coats with heavy buttons or belts are additionally effective because of their weight.

Pulling the wool over his eyes—push away to blind and distract.

Resist by whipping a heavy coat into the side of the head.

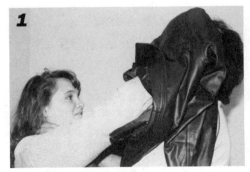

Throw coat over face, then spin attacker in circles to disorient.

Clothing
...Hat

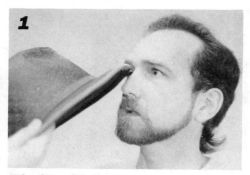

Flipping the hat brim into the eyes.

The brim of a hat placed accurately in the eyes can blind an assailant and cause total disorientation. Shoving a hat into his face can result in confusion and loss of balance, allowing other attacks, such as a knee to the groin or use of other Implement Weapons, or enabling you to escape.

Pushing top of hat into the face to obscure attacker's vision and confuse him.

Clothing
...Gloves

Slapping an attacker with a pair of gloves is not as impractical as it may seem. The whipping action and noise will confuse and disorient him. This technique would be effective when timed as an immediate reaction to the attack as a means to escape. It could also be used to create distraction as you execute a more injurious technique.

Wearing gloves will protect and support your hands, giving you greater confidence and power if you punch the attacker.

Clothing
...Hair clips

Hair accessories are often made of hard plastic which can quickly be broken to create razor-sharp edges. Most pieces can be used for jabbing into vital areas such as the eyes, throat, and groin.

For centuries, women have used articles worn in their hair to defend themselves. Hat pins and hair pins have always been very popular for this purpose.

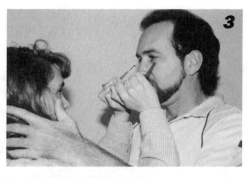

Headband tips thrust into the eyes.

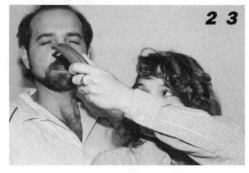

Banana clip jabbed over the shoulder into attacker's face.

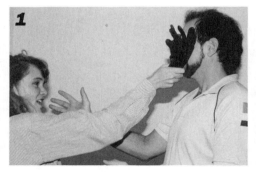

Violently whip a pair of gloves back and forth across the attacker's face to show immediate reaction and resistance.

Clothing
...Undergarments

Choking with a bra twisted around neck.

Chances are, if your undergarments have been removed and are available for use as weapons, your privacy is definitely threatened. There are other situations, however, where these clothing items may be located, such as in the laundry or in luggage. The material in these garments is strong and may be used much like a rope for binding and choking.

Gain distance from the attacker by pushing him away with a brassiere.

Women's purses are
usually brimming over
with a variety of items,

Purse Items

almost all of which may be implemented as weapons.
As you saw illustrated in the section, *Clothing*, the
purse itself may also be used in defending yourself.

Generally, items from your purse would have to
be removed in advance of a self-defense situation; for
example, you might prepare to walk across a darkened
parking lot with a nail file or car keys at the ready. In
other cases, you may have to manipulate the situation
to gain access to the items. The photos in this chapter
will help you recognize the potential Implement
Weapons available to you nearly everywhere you go.

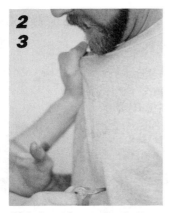

2
3

Firmly grip a single key in fingers and stab into heart area.

Purse Items
...Keys

The use of keys as weapons has long been suggested, especially when going to and from your car or home. You should always have your keys ready in advance—a woman fumbling to find a key or get it into the lock makes a vulnerable target.

Keys will generally be used for stabbing, though hitting an assailant with them can be equally effective. Keys flung at the face can cause serious injury to the eyes, and at the very least could cause sufficient pain and confusion to permit your escape or follow-up attack.

3

Poking tips of keys into the eyes.

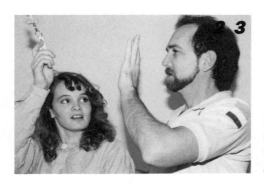

3

Holding on to a long key chain and slapping the keys across the attacker's face.

Purse Items
...Nail file and clippers

A nail file can be used to stab an attacker anywhere you can reach, and its small size gives you a good opportunity to create surprise and confusion. This kind of technique can obviously inflict first, second, or third degree injuries, and could even prove to be fatal.

The file on a pair of clippers can be used in the same ways as a regular nail file. Additionally, the sharp edges of the clippers can be used to tear skin by raking across sensitive areas, such as wrist, inner forearm, groin, etc.

Sharp edge of clippers will cut arm, allowing escape or other attack.

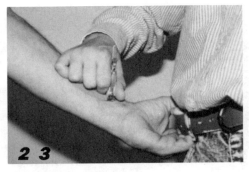

Raking the sharp cutting edges of clippers across wrist.

Stabbing nail file into eyes or face.

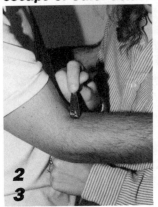

Stabbing nail file into the heart area.

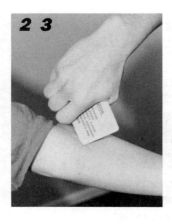

Cutting soft skin of inner elbow with plastic I.D. card.

Purse Items
...License & cards

Laminated cards, like your driver's license or I.D. card, can be gripped firmly without injury to your hands, while their sharp edges can be used to cut or slice the wrists, throat, or other vital areas of an assailant. The hard plastic of credit cards may also be used for cutting or striking the attacker.

The appearance of blood, however superficial the wound, will create momentary shock, allowing your escape or further defense. As an immediate response, it can discourage the attacker from continuing at all.

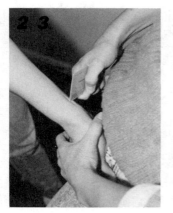

(above) **Laminated driver's license or stiff plastic card thrust deeply into the throat.**

Cutting downward across an attacker's wrist will likely make him release his grip!

Purse Items
...Make-up applicator

Make-up and applicators come in a variety of shapes and sizes. Most of them have sharp points or tips which are applied as weapons by poking or stabbing. Regular inkpens and pencils, also to be found in your purse, can be used in the same fashion.

The corners of hard plastic make-up cases, such as eye shadows and blush, can be used for striking targets such as the temple.

Eyeliner or brow pencil easily penetrates the eye.

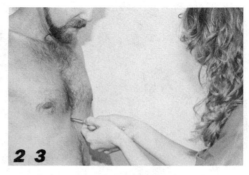

Lipstick brush jabbed into area of the heart.

Purse Items
...Coins

Perhaps all you have to defend yourself is a handful of coins. Anything is a weapon! Coins, particularly heavy ones like silver dollars, flung at the face, can cause quite a bit of pain and confusion. A roll of coins held within your fist will add power to your punch.

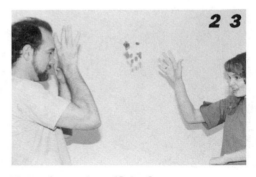

Throwing a handful of coins shows resistance to an attack.

Even the sweetest scent may drive away an assailant if sprayed into his eyes.

Purse Items
...Sprays and powders

Temporarily blinding an attacker may provide you with ample time to counter-attack or escape. Pump or aerosol sprays such as hairspray, perfume, or deodorant aimed into the eyes, or powder blown or thrown into the face would be quite surprising and painful. Some chemicals can even cause permanent damage to the eyes.

(left) **A bottle of powder squeezed firmly makes a blinding cloud.**

(below) **Hairspray can blind an attacker and impair his breathing.**

Blowing a handful of powder directly into the attacker's face.

Purse Items
...Dental floss

Dental floss is extremely strong nylon, even stronger when doubled. Some types are nearly impossible to break with your hands. This common item can cut through the skin with little effort and may also be used for grappling or tying.

Dental floss is doubled around fingers and pushes attacker back across his eyes.

When doubled, dental floss may be used with a sawing motion to cut the throat.

Purse Items
...Lighter

A cigarette lighter is an excellent weapon, as it can be concealed in the hand and the sudden light and heat of its flame will stun and possibly injure the assailant. It is a common enough item that it may openly be taken from the purse without alarming an attacker. A lit cigarette may also be used.

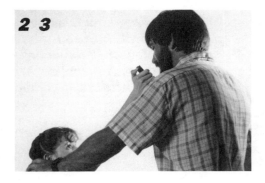

High flame of adjustable lighter wards off a potential assailant.

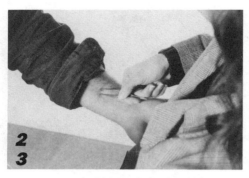

Apply firm pressure when pushing or pulling tweezers across the wrist.

Purse Items
...Tweezers

Although you probably won't be able to defend yourself by plucking out a man's eyebrows, tweezers do have some practical applications as an Implement Weapon.

The sharp corners on the tips can easily penetrate soft skin if firmly dragged or raked across it. They may also cause puncture wounds if used for striking, such as to the throat, heart area, or the eyes.

Taking a round-about approach to self-defense: Here, victim pretends compliance, then attacks to throat.

**1– Discomfort and distraction
2– Pain and minor injury
3– Injury requiring medical attention**

Purse Items
...Comb and brush

Certainly most women carry a comb or brush at all times. These can be used very subtly, as you can gain access to your weapon as you prepare (or pretend) to fix your hair. Various styles of combs and brushes may be used in different ways.

Pointed pieces such as a brush handle or rattail comb or pick are ideal for stabbing. Stiff bristles may be raked across the eyes or other sensitive areas. They may also be used for striking. Some of these techniques can be extremely damaging to the attacker.

The sharp "rat-tail" of a comb or pick can pierce the neck and the windpipe.

Raking a hairbrush across the eyes and face.

The handle of a pick or hairbrush thrust into the groin.

Large comb used to pull upward at groin.

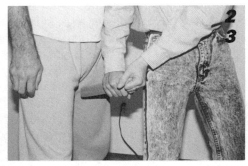

SCENE 1

Lisa had known him for a couple years, but this was the first time she had ever gone out with him. She didn't really know Brett that well, but he had seemed nice enough. So when he asked her out for a date, she agreed. They went out to dinner and had a great time. He was charming, and when he mentioned a special place where he liked to stargaze, she was enchanted.

A short time later they arrived at a cul-de-sac atop a small hill overlooking a pond. For a while the two of them just sat on the tailgate of his pickup, looking out at the sky and water. It was the perfect ending to a wonderful evening.

Lisa was watching the stars twinkle and dance when she felt Brett's hand begin to slowly slide up the inside of her thigh. Before he reached the hem of her miniskirt, she took his hand firmly in her own and held on to it. Realizing his initial attempt had failed, Brett decided to try a different tact. Putting his arm around her, he pulled her close and began kissing her neck and shoulder. She tried to pull away gently, but he wouldn't let her.

"Please stop," she asked. "Don't ruin this evening. We've had a good time." Brett seemed too engrossed with what he was doing to stop, so Lisa shoved him away. He looked at her.

"You must be kidding, Lisa. I know you want me. Stop being so difficult." With those words, Brett grabbed her shoulders and pushed her down into the bed of the truck. He began kissing and grabbing at her, ripping the top couple buttons from her blouse.

"Stop it! Stop!" she screamed. Her resistance only aroused him more, and Lisa knew she had to do something fast. She had a can of mace, but it was in her purse inside the cab of the truck. Using the large silver bracelet on her wrist, she twisted beneath Brett and managed to rake the sharp metal edges across the side of his face. Painful welts began to swell and a few small drops of blood trickled from them. Brett was violently angered and raised his fist, but before he could strike, Lisa backhanded him across the face. She felt her sapphire ring dig into his cheek. Brett felt it too, and reached up to touch the cut. He looked at the blood on his hand in shock.

That was just the moment Lisa needed. Using both hands, she shoved Brett off of her. He fell over the back of the truck and tumbled down the hill. Lisa jumped off the truck, grabbed her purse and took off for the lights of the nearest house.

At one time, I conducted
a self defense seminar for
an aerobics studio. As I
instructed grappling and release techniques, manipulating the hands and wrists, I noticed that, as usual, the ladies had a difficult time understanding and performing the techniques. It was nearly impossible for them to learn this advanced self defense in such a short period of time.

Jewelry

The *un*usual thing I noticed was that my hands and arms began to bleed from cuts made by the large, sharp rings some of the ladies had accidently touched me with. Most of the ladies attending wore exceptionally large rings and other fine jewelry, and it made me wonder if maybe I was teaching them the wrong thing, seeing as how I was injured by their jewelry with such little effort.

Most pieces of jewelry have hard surfaces with sharp edges—consider the diamond and other cut gems. Though these items may be small, don't underestimate their effectiveness in inflicting serious injury. Considering the convenient availability of your jewelry, these are among the easiest and most inconspicuous of Implement Weapons to use.

Forcefully stabbing with the clasp of a barette can penetrate the temple.

Jewelry
...Barrettes & hair clips

Letting your hair down is one way of acquiring an item with which to defend yourself. You might pretend cooperation or just subtly remove a hair clasp; in other confrontations, it might be the only thing within your reach.

The use of hair accessories as weapons will generally require quick and forceful execution, such as stabbing or striking. More ornate accessories, such as jeweled combs and clips, can be used for raking or scraping, as other jewelry included in this section.

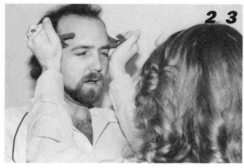

Hair combs grasped in both hands and raked down temples.

A hair clip poked into the eye can add distance between you and the assailant.

(right) Barrette clasp used as a knife to scrape and cut the soft skin of inner arm.

Jewelry
...Pendant or charm

Most necklace charms are made from gold or silver, although new fashions are bringing us jewelry of large, chunky plastic pieces. These may have strong, sharp edges. Some charms and pendants are shaped like spikes or have points which can be used for stabbing. Lockets can be opened to expose cutting edges. Some of these items might be used without removing them if they are on long necklaces and you are close enough to the target area.

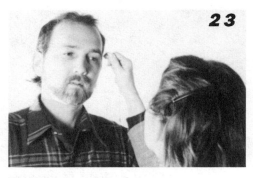

The sharp point of a heart-shaped pendant slicing across the attacker's temple.

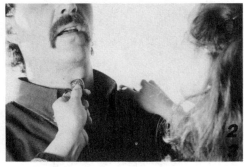

Sharp edge of a charm is pushed into neck and raked across skin.

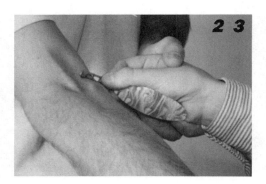

2
3

Even without removing them, earrings can be used to cut or puncture the skin.

Jewelry
...Earrings

Even the smallest objects are considered Implement Weapons. The tiny post of an earring made for pierced ears can be grasped firmly in the fingertips and used to cut or gouge. Clip-on earrings will also give you a cutting edge against an attacker. Dangling earrings or ones with jagged edges can be used to slice much like a knife. If you are close enough, you may be able to injure the attacker's face or neck without even removing the earring.

2
3

A discreet attack, such as an earring post used to stab or rake the neck, can shock as well as injure.

3

Pointed dangle earring poked over-the-shoulder into attacker's eye.

(right) Once removed, the earring can cause injury to other vital areas, like cutting the veins of the inner elbow.

Jewelry
...Bracelet

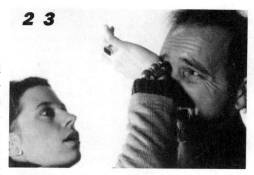

2 3

Bracelets of silver and turquoise or other combinations of metal and stone are popular today. As weapons, they are quite heavy, with sharp pieces or edges. Other current styles which can benefit women in self defense situations are heavy beaded bracelets and those made of multiple strands of beads or faux pearls.

Striking the eyes or facial area with a heavy bracelet.

Swinging your arms with hands back and striking with the wrist is most effective. Attack in such a manner to face or groin.

1– Discomfort and distraction
2– Pain and minor injury
3– Injury requiring medical attention

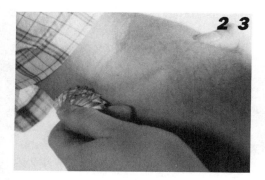

2 3

2 3

Jewelry
...Necklace

A heavy bead necklace whipped across eyes to blind and injure.

The lengths that necklaces range in are often just right to be swung at a target effectively. Heavy pearls or beads can break the skin and cause bleeding when swung accurately at the face. A strong gold chain can cut when grasped at each end and raked across the neck, or wrapped and twisted tightly around the throat, arm, or leg.

1 2

A strong strand of pearls raked across his eyes pushes the attacker away.

Consider also the possibility of using your necklace without removing it. If an attacker has grabbed your shoulder or neck, you may be able to break his grip by cutting his wrist.

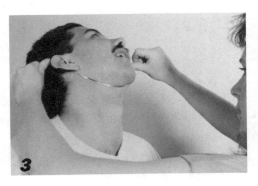

A heavy, smooth chain can cut into throat when firmly pushed and raked across.

(right) Similar action can be taken against the wrist, or the inner elbow, or groin.

3

Jewelry
...Watch

Some watches have sharp corners and edges along with sharp metal bands. Their application as an Implement Weapon is similar to that of bracelets and armlets, although they may be capable of causing greater damage.

Using the back of your hand, rake your wristwatch across the face.

Jewelry
...Broach

The use of the broach will generally require it to be removed. The pin may be used like those of the badges in this section. Depending on its shape and material, the decorative item itself may also be used for poking, raking, and stabbing the target areas.

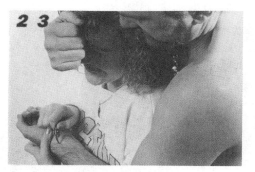

Gouging a half-moon shaped broach across the wrist to break the attacker's hold.

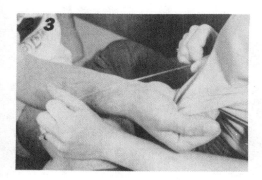

2

Jewelry
...Armlet

Another popular jewelry item is the armlet, a band of metal worn either at the wrist or on the upper arm. Armlets can usually be bent into various shapes. A thin, open-end band can be straightened for stabbing or poking, or curved for hooking or gouging.

Though the sturdiness of a round or enclosed armlet will give slightly different results, its applications are similar to those of the bracelet and watch.

Armlet hooked under nose pushes face back, allowing escape or additional attack.

2

Hooking the end of an armlet into the neck and pulling upward.

2
3

The armlet is held by spreading fingers, and the sharp edge is raked across face.

(right) Straightened end of an armlet is used to blind the attacker.

Jewelry
...Badge

Buttons and badges are fairly common—worn for fun or sported on backpacks, given for nametags at meetings and conventions, even worn to advertise specials in retail stores and restaurants. These handy items come equipped with a built-in weapon—the pin— and they are easily and discreetly removed.

The effectiveness of this weapon is obvious.

Victim with arm around attacker's neck, unexpectedly stabbing to injure and confuse him.

Jabbing into an attacker's arm to break his grip.

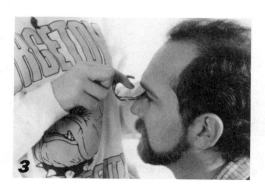

Jewelry
...Rings

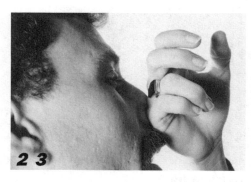

Punch with the jeweled ring and rake it across throat.

The diamond is the world's hardest material. Its cut edges can be very sharp and dangerous. Other cut stones can be equally effective for defending yourself.

The mounting prongs of the rings add to the cutting effect, while the weight of large rings can damage the face when properly used for striking.

Rings are pictured here, both worn normally and turned around into the palm, raking across the face and eyes. Remember to apply them to other vital areas such as the wrist or groin.

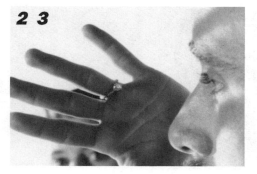

Backhand slap a heavy or jeweled ring to the temple or eyes.

Turn the gem around into palm and drag hand across the face.

Paper Products

As strange as it may seem, paper items can become deadly weapons.

I'm sure all of us have had a paper cut at one time or another and have noticed how painful and distracting such a small injury can be. The use of a magazine or newspaper to inflict these wounds on an assailant will stun and surprise him. In addition, the noise of paper as it is whipped across the face and eyes can shock and confuse him, demonstrating your resistance to his attack and possibly ending the confrontation.

Do not underestimate the potential of inflicting physical damage with everyday paper items—there is actually a type of training in which students learn to throw cards from a new deck (with stiff, crisp, sharp edges) in such a way that they can penetrate the skin or even penetrate into the body.

Paper Products
...Newspaper

The newspaper is very effective for disorienting and confusing an assailant. The sudden blindness you can create, along with the noise, can deter the attack. A folded newspaper can be whipped back and forth across the face, adding the potential of injury as well.

Immediate reaction—shove an open newspaper into his face.

Paper Products
...Books

Books applied as Implement Weapons offer several options. The corners of hardcover books and the bound spines of paperbacks can severely injure the eyes, temple, or groin. They can be shoved corner- or spine-first into the face or heart area. They can also be thrown. Heavy books carry extra momentum, and swinging a thick book into the side of the head could render the attacker unconscious.

Corner of a hardback book striking into the heart area.

Hard, sharp corner of a book can tear the skin and even break bone when used to forcefully strike the temple.

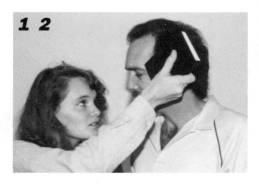

Paper Products
...Magazine

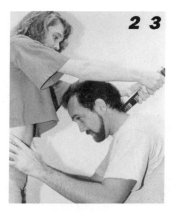

If your magazine is open, as if you were reading it, the top edges of the pages can be made into a knife-like weapon by grasping each side and firmly pulling outward on the pages. This technique can definitely cut the attacker as you whip the pages across his skin.

When a magazine is tightly rolled, it becomes almost as hard as the tree the paper was made from. The roll may be used in thrusting motions to attack the groin, heart area and other vital targets.

Striking with rolled-up magazine downward to the base of the skull.

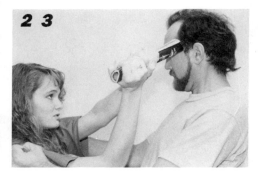

Jabbing attacker's temple with a rolled-up magazine. The eye is also a good target.

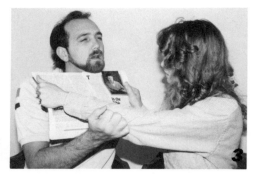

Pushing edges of open magazine into the neck and quickly jerking across to cut skin.

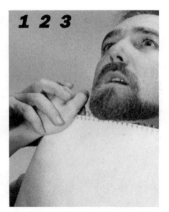

Raking the metal spiral across the throat.

Paper Products
...Spiral notebook

The coiled wire on these notebooks is made of stainless steel. The spiral itself can be used for raking across sensitive areas such as the eyes, face, or throat. The tip of the wire can be pulled out of the end and will scratch or cut. More wire may be pulled out of the pages for choking and grappling; another method of pulling the wire for this purpose is to tear the notebook in half across the middle, exposing the wire and allowing you a good grip on the pages.

Tip of wire poked into attacker's eye can cause serious damage.

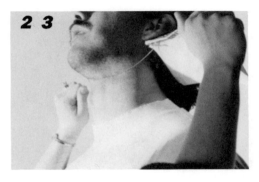

Wire pulled out from end and wrapped around neck.

Paper Products
...Photos

The paper on which photographs are printed is very stiff with sharp corners and edges. If the pictures are grasped firmly and raked across the skin, they can create deep cuts. The soft skin of the wrist and inner forearm, throat, or groin is especially vulnerable to this type of attack.

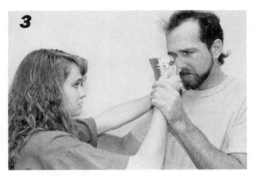

Poking the corners of photos into the eye.

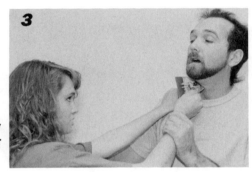

Even paper cuts may cause profuse bleeding from the throat.

Paper Products
...Phonebook

Telephone directories are readily accessible in the home or office. The weight of thick phone books can easily injure an attacker when the book is suddenly shoved into or swung back and forth across the face.

Corner of a phone directory shoved into the temple.

Paper Products
...Calendar

A calendar may be applied as a weapon much the same as a magazine. The calendar is included to remind you that paper items hanging on a wall may be at your disposal when nothing else is, and that these items too may serve as weapons of self defense.

A flat desk calendar could be implemented in a fashion similar to that of the newspaper.

Grasping sides of the calendar, push in and slice across the neck.

A rolled-up calendar swung up into groin helps you escape.

Paper Products
...Envelopes

The thinness and flexibility of an envelope would require a very quick cutting motion, but if done properly, the edge will slice like a razor. Use the element of surprise.

Paper Products
...File folder

Cuts from the crisp edges of new file folders are among the most irritating and painful of paper cuts. Manilla folders are common in the office or home, and are made of good, stiff paper. Individual folders can make deep paper cuts.

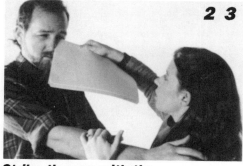

Strike the eye with the corner of a file folder to blind the attacker.

The use of a stack of folders is like that of several other Implement Weapons, such as the hardcover and paperback books, the phone book, or magazines.

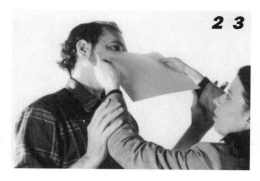

Top edge of a manilla folder easily cuts across the face.

(left) Use gummed flap of envelope to slice across neck.

(right) Sharp edge of flap cuts across the attacker's wrist.

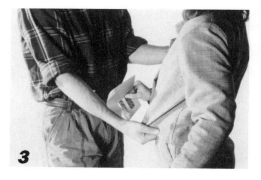

2 3

A playing card raked across the wrist can penetrate veins and arteries.

3

Use firm pressure to cut the throat with playing cards.

Paper Products
...Playing cards

This book *cannot* teach you killing throwing techniques with a deck of cards. You can, however, learn to defend yourself from attack with one.

A new deck of playing cards has sharp, cut edges. They are thin and usually plastic coated for stiffness. You can use the corners and edges to shock and injure an attacker by cutting his wrist, throat, or other tender, vital areas.

Corner of card can penetrate surface veins of inner forearm.

Car Items

Many crimes against women occur in or around automobiles. News reports tell often of women being forced into vehicles and abducted, or becoming victims when they are forced into passenger seats as their own cars are stolen. Women are vulnerable to attack while seeking road-side assistance for flat tires or engine trouble. With the mounting incidence of "acquaintance rape", there is even danger associated with dating and carpooling.

With this in mind, companies are now offering alarms for automobiles which can be activated by a hand-held switch within a certain distance of the car. Auto makers also are equipping cars with these devices, some of which will even turn on headlights and blow the horn.

Several of the items appearing in this chapter may seem totally impractical to use in self defense. As an alternative to becoming a helpless, submissive victim, however, the use of these Implement Weapons can be made quite effective.

Floor mat used to beat abductor about the head and face.

Rolled-up floor mat thrusting to groin.

Car Items
...Floor mats

Floor mats are commonly made of a heavy rubber or vinyl material and are generally accessible from either the front or back seats.

A floor mat might be reached without raising suspicion in the attacker and used to strike quite suddenly. In cases of car theft and abduction, the victim might use a floor mat to beat the thief about his face to make him unable to continue driving; it certainly would draw the attention of anyone nearby.

In a remote location or at night, a self defense technique would probably have to inflict a higher degree injury. A floor mat rolled up becomes a stiff tube for thrusting to the heart or groin. Held with an end in each hand, it can be pressed across the throat or eyes to push attacker away.

1– Discomfort and
    distraction
2– Pain and minor
    injury
3– Injury requiring
    medical attention

Car Items
...Seatbelt

Seatbelts are also found in both the front and back seats. The strong webbing might be used to choke an assailant, or the buckle used to strike areas such as the temple or throat.

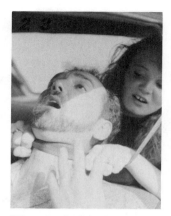

Woman in back seat choking driver with seat belt.

Choking driver with seat belt from front passenger seat.

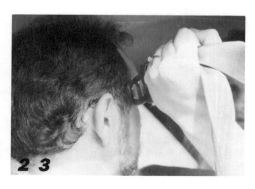

Striking temple with seatbelt buckle.

Car Items
...Ice scraper

The ice scraper offers specific advantages when applied as an Implement Weapon. First, it already has a handle. Second it has a sharp scraping edge and corners made to break up ice. It also is an extension of the arm, giving you a longer reach.

Corner of ice scraper attacking to heart.

Sharp corner of ice scraper slicing across throat.

Car Items
...Ashtray

The ashtray, if you smoke, contains a secret weapon: ashes. These blinding little particles can be thrown or blown into the eyes. The removable tray itself is a weapon for striking or raking across the skin.

Car Items
...Plastic straw

It's hard to tell just what has gathered in the glove box or floor of your car. One common item is a drinking straw. If you place your thumb over the end or bend the straw so the air inside cannot escape, the straw will penetrate skin or eyes as easily as a pen or pencil. Be quick, forceful, and accurate.

A plastic straw can penetrate into the area of the heart.

Plastic drinking straw jabbed into abductor's throat.

(left) **Ashes will temporarily blind an attacker when blown into his eyes.**

(right) **Use the sharp corners and edges of an ashtray to strike to face and eyes.**

Car Items
...Light bulb and lens

Dome light lens used to scrape and cut upward on the neck.

The lens (cover) of an auto courtesy or dome light is readily removable. The hard plastic edge may be firmly scraped across the skin of the face, neck, wrist or groin. Breaking the lens into pieces will yield sharp cutting edges.

Likewise, the light bulb may be removed and broken. The sharp glass remaining in the socket can cause severe damage to the same areas.

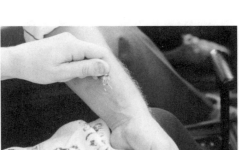

Cutting wrists with the broken bulb to release abductor's grip.

Car Items
...Cigarette lighter

Though you may not have considered this item for self defense, its use is obvious! If you smoke, you could easily light a cigarette, then use the lighter to burn almost any part of the attacker's body. If you don't smoke, fake it.

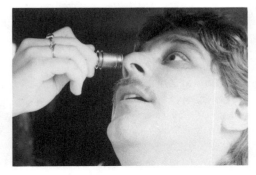

Auto cigarette lighter aimed directly into attacker's face.

Car Items
...Mirror

If approached or attacked in a car, you have access to the rear-view mirror or mirrors which may be in your purse or glove box. The hard glass and casing of the rear-view mirror make it an excellent tool for striking, though you may go through some trouble to remove it.

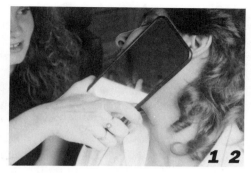

Hard casing of mirror striking back into face.

Car Items
...Whiskbroom

A whiskbroom may be at your fingertips, under the seat or in the glove box. The stiff bristles cause extreme discomfort and can penetrate when thrust into or firmly brushed across the skin. An attack to the eyes can cause temporary blindness or permanent damage.

Jamming whiskbroom bristles into eyes.

Car Items
...Antenna

If you are attacked near a car, an antenna may be within reach. The flexible metal rod may be snapped off and used like a fencing sword to whip back and forth and to stab. Remember the antenna of a portable radio as well.

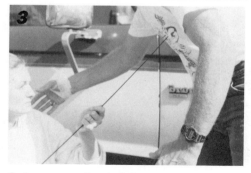

Antenna end used to gouge into heart area.

SCENE 2

Janet stepped off the curb in front of her health club, wiping the sweat from her forehead. Hanging the towel around her neck and adjusting her gym bag on her shoulder, she started across the asphalt. All she could think about was home, a cool shower, and some dinner.

It was dusk, and as usual, her car was at the far end of the parking lot. She had covered half the distance to it when she heard a car door open and close. This didn't bother her, though. What did concern her was the sound of heavy footsteps rushing up from behind.

She glanced back over her shoulder to see who was there. The rapidly approaching man was taller and quite a bit bigger, and he was staring right at her. Janet broke into a run toward her car.

She heard his steps getting closer and reached up to grab the end of her towel. His large hand fell on her shoulder and she immediately spun around, whipping the towel from around her neck and across the eyes of her attacker. He staggered back, covering his face. Janet quickly let her bag slip from her shoulder. She caught the strap in her hand and swung the bag in an upward arc toward his crotch. His hands dropped from his face to his groin as his knees buckled. Groaning, he fell to the pavement.

Janet took a quick look at her assailant, so she could later describe him to the police. She pulled her keys from the bag and ran to the safety of her car.

A most popular activity **Exercise Gear**
of women today is exercise
and fitness. Crimes against
women may occur while they are on their way to or
from their exercise, or possibly within the workout
facility itself. This may be particularly true of outdoor
locations such as tennis courts or secluded fitness
trails and jogging and cycling paths.

There are usually specific items that accompany
women for certain types of activities. Everything you
might carry for your workout sessions, from a towel to
analgesic rub, can in some way aid you in self defense. Included here are some of the most common
items.

Stopwatch cord pulled across attacker's eyes from behind.

Exercise gear
...Stopwatch

A stopwatch is quite handy for runners and cyclists, and for interval training and checking heart rates. It is also quite handy to surprise your attacker with a sudden defense.

The stopwatch or pedometer has a hard plastic casing which can be swung at the face or held in the hand for striking. The cord may be applied as a weapon when used to choke, rake or push across the eyes, or grapple with the hands.

Stopwatch swung at eyes or temple.

Exercise gear
...Weights

Small dumbells are a comfortable extension of the hand. They can cause severe damage to the face, temple, or groin. Flexible ankle weights could be swung at the face; both types could be thrown.

Exercise gear
...Resistance band

Rubber bands and surgical tubing, which provide resistance for muscle toning, are used in many aerobics programs. They make good weapons with their strength and the way they bind the skin. Your exercise band could be used to push an attacker away, to choke him, or to entangle his hands or feet. Like a big rubber band, it could also be snapped to the eyes.

Resistance band used to choke from behind.

Exercise band pushes entire face back and blocks breathing.

(left) **Hand weight swung backward and upward into groin.**

(right) **Even a light dumbell can knock out an attacker if used to strike the temple.**

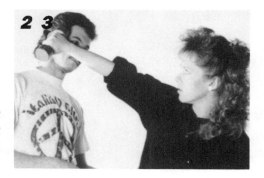

To break attacker's grip, bend down and swing exercise mat backwards to the groin.

Exercise gear
...Floor-work mats

Your cumbersome exercise mat which you faithfully tote back and forth to each aerobics class might someday come to your rescue. Rolled tightly, it may be swung at the attacker's face to cause confusion and show your resistance, though no real injury is likely to occur.

Shoving the rolled mat forcefully up under the chin, into the face, or into the groin could injure and disorient the assailant long enough for you to escape or follow up with a more severe attack.

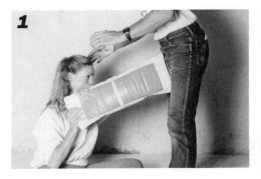

End of rolled mat shoved upward from ground, striking groin.

1– Discomfort and
    distraction
2– Pain and minor
    injury
3– Injury requiring
    medical attention

Exercise gear
...Gym bag

Your gym bag is an excellent weapon for self defense. In addition to its availability for immediate reaction to a threatening approach, it is often filled with heavy items such as weights, shoes, bottles of shampoo, etc.

The exact application may vary depending on the bag's size, shape, and length of handles. The bag can be swung to the front or behind. It can also be shoved into vital areas.

Gym bag suddenly thrust at throat.

Victim turns back and swings bag at face.

Shoving bag forward into groin.

2
3

Cassette tape player jabbed backward into assailant's groin.

Exercise gear
...Pocket radio/tape player

Everyone working out seems to want to escape with their own music. These small tape players, radios, and now CD players can be used in a variety of ways as Implement Weapons.

Many items in this book have similar construction of hard plastic and sharp edges or corners. These portable music players and the cassette tapes or CDs in them may all be used for striking vital targets. With the headphone cords, you can choke or grapple your assailant.

2
3

Portable radio suddenly thrust into temple.

Exercise gear
...Sprays

Busy people often leave their exercise club or class to return to work or some other activity. Grooming items you might carry back and forth would include hairspray and spray deodorants and perfumes. These chemicals would be just as effective as the traditional Mace® spray in warding off an attacker. They will obviously work best when sprayed into the eyes.

Remember, though, the purpose of this book is to teach you that anything

Aerosol deodorant sprayed into eyes.

is a weapon. What if you can't spray to the eyes or the valve clogs? As other items in this book, the spray container (bottle or can) itself may be used to throw, strike, or thrust at the attacker.

Exercise gear
...Towel

Your towel can be used in ways similar to several of the clothing items. It can be used to whip across the face to create confusion or to push an attacker away from yourself. Another method would be to grasp an end firmly in each hand, push into face across eyes and nose, and then jerk rapidly to the side (continue pushing, as in a buffing motion).

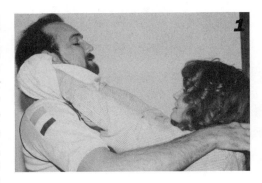

Towel used in choking to break assailant's grip and push away.

Sweatband thrust around neck, choking and pushing away.

Exercise gear
...Sweatband

Sweatbands and elastic headbands are of strong, elastic material. They can be used to push the assailant away and break his hold. A sweatband can cause extreme discomfort when it is hooked through the thumbs and thrust around neck, across eyes, or even up under the nose.

Analgesic rub squeezed directly into eyes.

Exercise gear
...Analgesic Rub

A muscle heat-rub squeezed into an attacker's eyes will definitely disable him, allowing you to escape. An equal effect may be obtained by applying the ointment into the nose or mouth. Any victim of boys' locker-room antics will also attest to its affectiveness when applied to the groin!

Household Items

The home could be one of the last places a woman would ever expect to have to defend or protect herself. Unfortunately, many reported violent crimes occur in the home, including the crimes of rape, date or acquaintance rape, and most cases of abuse. Beyond traditional protection such as alarms, dogs, guns or even your telephone, the average home contains a great variety of Implement Weapons.

Try to imagine your home without kitchen knives, sewing scissors, garden shears, and other utility tools—you probably can't picture it. Many homes are also "protected" by guns. As obvious and effective as these things are as weapons, they may not be readily available or you may lack the confidence to use them. And these tools will work just as well against you in the hands of an assailant.

The things closest at hand are the items to learn to use as weapons. With training, imagination, and common sense, a multitude of Implement Weapons are right at your fingertips.

Household Items
...Curtainrod

Pulling your curtains down and breaking the window will likely deter attack as it draws attention from neighbors. The curtains can then be used as a net to slow and confuse the attacker. The rods may be swung or jabbed at vital areas.

Curtain rod thrust deeply into heart area.

Household Items
...Lightbulbs and lamps

Lamps are classic weapons in movie fight scenes. But consider their advantage as Implement Weapons: lightbulbs get very hot, very quickly. Remove the shade from a nearby lamp and use the bulb to burn the attacker. The sudden, bright light thrust into his face will temporarily blind him.

A broken lightbulb is also useful. Its tiny glass shards will cut. If the lamp is plugged in and the switch on, the exposed filaments give a strong electric shock.

Hot lightbulb swung against the side of the face, quickly burning tender skin.

Hot, bright bulb thrust to face blinds attacker.

Household Items
...Dishes & decorations

Many homes are adorned with ashtrays, candy dishes and other knick-knacks. Heavy glass and metal pieces are available in almost any room. The variety of their shapes and sizes lends them to swinging, striking, raking and stabbing. Broken glass dishes may be pulled firmly across the skin, slicing with the sharp exposed edges.

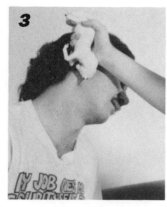

This sharp, pointed knick-knack is ideal for stabbing into throat.

Scrambling from the floor, find a weapon, such as this glass figurine, and attack to neck.

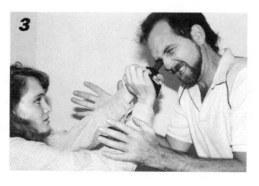

Candle and holder deeply penetrate attacker's eye.

Household Items
...Telephone

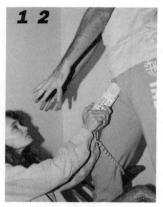

Fend off attacker by striking to groin with telephone handset.

In nearly every place in the home where an attack might occur, there is a telephone nearby—in the kitchen, by the couch, on the bedside table, maybe even the bathroom! Your portable phone goes anywhere you do.

The hard plastic handset and base of the phone are employed in striking or thrusting to vital areas. The cord may be used to choke, push attacker away, or for tying hands or feet.

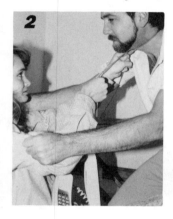

Wrapping phone cord around neck and pulling to choke.

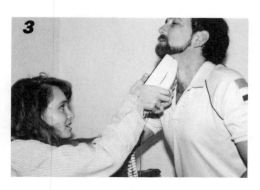

Accurate attack to larynx can cause serious damage.

Household Items
...Videos, Tapes & CDs

These handy items are stored in hard, plastic cases with sharp corners and edges. Cassette and compact disk boxes are effective weapons for striking, and the sharp corners may be raked over the skin. The box could be broken, making extremely sharp edges for cutting or stabbing.

The larger video tape cases would be used in the same way as the cassette boxes. Additionally, they could be grasped in both hands and thrust into vital areas such as the groin or throat. The cassettes themselves can be used to strike, and CD edges to slice.

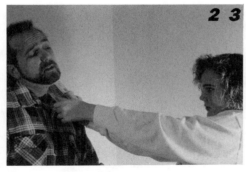

Corner of tape box shoved into the neck.

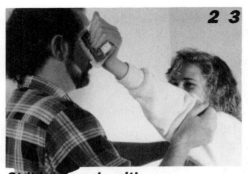

Striking temple with corner of cassette box.

Household Items
...Plants and Pots

Another domestic fight cliché is the flowerpot-over-the-head. Comic as it is, it's still a viable alternative to attack. The leaves of some houseplants provide weapons: for example, spiny cactus or palm trees.

Plant pot and cactus shoved into groin.

From the floor, a folding seat is pushed into the groin.

Household Items
...Tables and chairs

Defending yourself with a small chair or table will give you the advantage of keeping out of the attacker's grasp even as you are able to reach him with your Implement Weapon. Thrusting or shoving the table or chair legs at the attacker is effective. If the furniture is broken, the pieces also can be used in the same way.

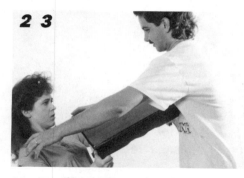

Small end table used to force attacker away and break his grasp.

1– Discomfort and
    distraction
2– Pain and minor
    injury
3– Injury requiring
    medical attention

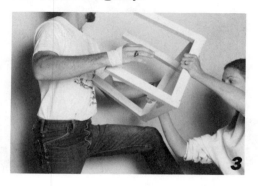

Small table leg jabbed into the area of the heart.

Household Items
...Cushion, blanket, or pillow

As you learned as a child, or maybe as a parent, fighting with a blanket or pillow will not cause severe injury. These items may be used simply as a deterent to allow other forms of defense or escape, and to make a show of resistance. The noise and violent motion can prevent the attacker's actions and may give you time to flee the house.

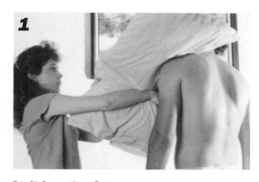

Striking the face with a pillow to create surprise and confusion.

Smothering with a pillow or blanket will force the assailant to back off.

Blanket thrown over attacker's head to blind and disorient him.

Household Items
...Clock
or radio

An alarm clock or clock radio are generally just an arm's length from the bed. This item could be used to rapidly strike the attacker. If applied forcefully to the temple, the blow could knock him out.

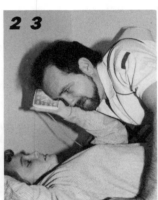

(above) **Pushing attacker off by thrusting clock up into his throat.**

Rapid striking with sharp corner of clock to the temple.

Household Items
...Picture
frame

A picture can quickly be taken from the wall or tabletop and swung at an attacker. Use sharp corners of small or medium frames in striking or raking. Larger frames can distance you from the assailant. Broken glass can be used to cut.

Suddenly attacking to groin with the corner of a picture frame.

I had been a long, rough day at work, and Sandi didn't look forward to the ride home in the rain. Looking out the window at the downpour, she gathered her purse and umbrella and locked up her office. The building was empty save for an occasional janitor.

SCENE 3

Waiting for the elevator, Sandi noticed an unfamiliar man coming down the hall to the lobby. He stopped, and Sandi could feel his eyes on her as she turned to step into the elevator. He smiled as he followed, and the doors closed behind them.

"This has got to be the slowest elevator," Sandi said, trying to make small talk.

"I don't mind," the man replied, leering. "Not at all." As the elevator inched its way down from the 19th floor, he took a step behind Sandi and placed his hand on her thigh.

"Excuse me!" she snorted, and abruptly moved away. Her face flushed with anger.

"No problem," came his answer, as he closed the space between them. With a threatening look, he reached out to grab her shoulders.

Sandi, holding her umbrella in both hands, swung it hard into his temple. The man staggered back, and Sandi tried to follow up with a swing at his groin. The man was faster. He caught the umbrella, wrenched it from her hands and threw it aside.

Sandi turned to find the elevator's emergency button, but the stranger had grabbed her from behind and was holding her tightly in a bear hug. She found his pinky finger and bent it cruelly back, as she scraped the heel of her shoe down the man's shin and slammed it into his instep. The man loosened his grip and Sandi whirled around, bringing her knee up into the man's groin. He collapsed on the floor.

The elevator slid open. Sandi snatched her umbrella, punched the 19th floor on the elevator, and stepped out as the doors closed behind her with her attacker trapped inside.

Office and Work

Graduating from school doesn't mean the end of homework! Traveling to and from their jobs, women are often weighed down with office materials and everyday work items. There are many office products which seem practical to use as Implement Weapons against an attacker.

Whether the incident might involve an unknown intruder or unwanted advances (or downright abuse) from a co-worker, remember that almost anything around you can be used to defend yourself and inflict injury when applied properly and accurately.

Stabbing pen into the heart.

Office and Work
...Pens and pencils

The utility of pens and pencils as weapons is obvious. Their sharp tips will penetrate any of the vital targets; eyes are especially vulnerable. With forceful, accurate application, they can even become deadly.

Sturdy briefcase swung backwards, striking with corner to groin.

Office and Work
...Briefcase

While on your way to and from work, you may frequently carry a briefcase or satchel under your arm. These items become Implement Weapons when swung at the attacker or shoved into the face or groin. The weight of a soft satchel can knock a man off balance, while the flat, portfolio-style case provides a strong striking edge and corner to attack throat, face, or groin.

Attacking from the floor, corner of the briefcase is shoved upwards into the groin.

Office and Work
...Umbrella

Carrying an umbrella is as common as a rainy day. The umbrella has a multitude of applications as a weapon. There are several martial arts styles which incorporate umbrella and cane fighting and self defense techniques.

The pointed tip of the umbrella can obviously be used for poking and stabbing. The crooked handle can be used to swiftly jerk an attacker's leg out from under him or attack to the groin. The straight handle, found on the newer, collapsible umbrellas, can be swung or shoved at vital targets such as the face, heart, or groin.

Swinging umbrella upwards to groin.

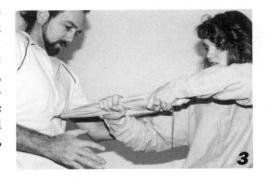

Stabbing tip of umbrella into heart.

This weapon even works when raised, or it can suddenly be opened to cause confusion. Here, victim flails umbrella into attacker's face and stabs with pointed end.

Office and Work
...Stapler

Swinging stapler to the temple can break the skin and draw blood.

Staplers come in a variety of sizes; all can be made into effective weapons. The smaller "mini" staplers fit neatly in the palm of the hand and tend to have sharp metal and plastic edges. They can be used to puncture or rake across the skin or stab or poke into the eyes.

The weight of the larger business staplers makes them effective when swung or thrust into vital areas. Also consider its weight as an effective projectile for throwing—an attacker who is pelted by every available object will have a hard time gaining physical control of his victim.

Thrusting small end of stapler into the heart area.

Swinging back and upward to the groin.

Office and Work
...Clipboard

This item is commonly on hand in the office and is often carried back and forth to work. The hard board can be used for striking across and in an up-and-down motion, or for thrusting and pushing attacker away from yourself. The metal endpiece can cut when used in a raking or slicing motion or if used to strike areas like the temple or throat.

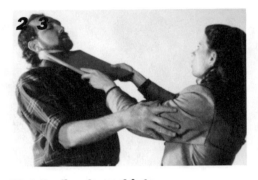

Metal clip shoved into attacker's throat.

Corner of clipboard shoved into the area of assailant's heart.

Office and Work
...Calculator

This desk-top or pocket item is usually at your fingertips. Its hard surfaces and corners make an effective Implement Weapon with which to resist attack.

Pocket calculator striking downward to face.

2 3

Corner of 5-1/4" disk
and folder being raked
across neck.

2 3

Use a 3-1/2" disk to
strike or cut the
temple.

Office and Work
...Computer diskette

Nearly every office is now computerized to some degree. With confident and rapid execution, even the computer "floppy" disks can inflict serious damage in your defense.

The $5\frac{1}{4}$- inch disk and its card-stock folder have sharp corners which can be pushed and dragged across sensitive areas such as the wrist and throat. The folder itself can be used in the same fashion as several of the "Paper Products" items.

The $3\frac{1}{2}$- inch diskettes are encased in hard plastic which can be used for striking vital targets.

Office and Work
...File box

Boxes for card files or computer disks can quickly be grabbed from the desktop. Corners of small, metal card boxes can be especially damaging when used to strike the face or temple.

2 3

Office and Work
...Push-pin

Sometimes, the smallest weapons can be the most effective. A tiny push-pin should not be underestimated as a weapon, as its small size will allow for unexpected attack. Its application as a weapon is likely to cause complete confusion because the assailant won't be able to identify it.

The push-pin can be used, obviously, for stabbing. Once it penetrates the skin, it can be raked or pulled through to result in a rather deep and nasty cut.

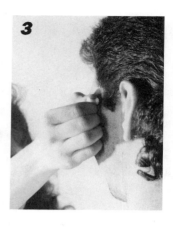

Push-pin penetrating into temple.

Push-pin will easily puncture the soft skin on the neck.

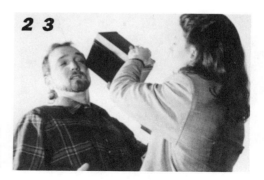

(left) Victim swings file box corner behind into attacker's groin.

(right) Metal file box corner is swung across to strike temple.

Office and Work
...Paper clip

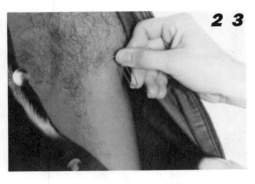

Straightened to give a sharp end, paper clip can poke an eye...

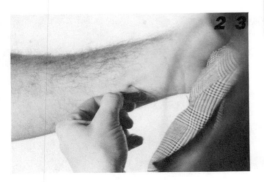

...stab into the heart area...

The paper clip is another of the "small but effective" Implement Weapons. It is basically a stainless steel wire which is very sharp and hard, but easily straightened to create a weapon for gouging, poking, or scratching across the skin. It is readily accessible and can be concealed in the palm of your hand.

Obvious targets include the throat, eyes and wrists. An attack to the groin area is also possible with this tiny weapon.

1– Discomfort and distraction
2– Pain and minor injury
3– Injury requiring medical attention

...or be pulled into skin of wrist, and more.

Natural Body

Martial arts teaches the application of the "empty" body as a weapon. The use of your body in self defense has almost innumerable possibilities. Striking areas or weapons which are most effective for women include, but are not limited to, the fingers and fingernails, palm and back of hand, elbow, knee, and parts of the foot. However, with an alert decision and accurate execution, the wrists, shins, toes, forearms, and even the hair can become your weapons for self defense.

The uses depicted here are among the most practical and easiest to learn. Repeating the techniques and actions will dramatically improve your accuracy and execution, thereby increasing the confidence and effectiveness of your defense.

Fingernails digging into the attacker's neck.

Natural Body
...Fingers & fingernails

Fingers and nails apply as weapons at times when nothing else will, as in very close quarters, in the dark, or when a victim is pinned and can't move anything else.

Fingers and fingernails are ideal for gouging the eyes, throat, groin, and even into the heart. The popular sculptured nails seem specifically designed to pierce the skin!

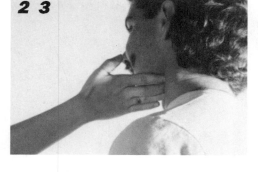

Fingertip "spearhand" attack goes deep into throat.

Natural Body
...Knuckles

A pointed knuckle attack is formed by tightly compacting the fingers, bending at the first knuckle. This position concentrates the power of a strike onto a small area, and is effective when focused at the groin, neck, or heart area.

Knuckle attack does damage to the groin.

Natural Body
...Open hand

Both the palm and the back of the hand may be applied as natural Implement Weapons. You may fend off an attacker or force him away by covering his eyes with your hand, squeezing, and pushing his whole face back, a technique requiring good confidence.

Open hand squeezing and pushing face back shows resistance and breaks attacker's grip.

Striking with the heel of the hand allows a woman to put all her power into the attack without the risk of injury to hand and wrist that can come from punching. The weapon is made by pulling the fingers and thumb back and aiming the palm heel at areas such as the jaw, nose, eyes, or groin.

Palm heel strike up under the nose causes injury and shock.

The back of the open hand also applies as a weapon. The knuckles will cause injury to the face or groin. Remember also that large rings will add results to this attack, even drawing blood or blinding the assailant.

Open backhand, rapping knuckles on the side of attacker's face.

Inner edge of forearm striking to temple.

Natural Body
...Forearm and wrist

Striking with the forearm or wrist will allow you to attack with power but require less accuracy than concentrated attacks with the knuckles or palm. The attack may be made by swinging arms in and across the front or out to the sides, striking the face, temple, or neck, or by swinging low to the groin. Remember that a watch or heavy bracelet may add weight to this self defense technique.

A sudden reaction: wrist striking down and back to groin.

1– Discomfort and
   distraction
2– Pain and minor
   injury
3– Injury requiring
   medical attention

Natural Body
...Knee

What woman wouldn't think to defend herself with a knee attack to the groin?! However, this technique becomes more effective when combined with another attack to distract the assailant and prevent him from protecting himself (for example, violently whipping a newspaper or purse across the face).

Add power to knee groin attack by jerking backs of upper arms.

Natural Body
...Elbow

Elbows, too, are excellent weapons for women. They are sharp, hard, and almost invulnerable when used to strike such targets as the temple, neck, heart area, or groin.

Another advantage of using elbow attacks in self defense is that they may be quickly executed in any number of direction: coming across in front; pushing outward to the sides; rising or dropping down; even attacking high or low to an attacker behind you.

Pushing elbow straight in to heart area.

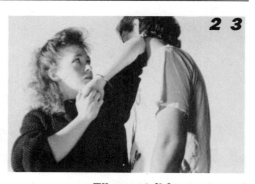

Elbow striking outward to neck and jaw.

Heel and bottom of foot attacking from the floor to the groin.

Natural Body
...Foot

The foot contains many striking areas, each of which may be applied in different ways and from different positions. Like other techniques, repeating the motions of these techniques over and over will result in dramatic improvement in speed, power, and accuracy.

Notice that several of these self defense techniques are performed barefoot; in other situations the effect will be aided by heavy or hard-soled shoes or boots.

Striking upward with the heel to the groin.

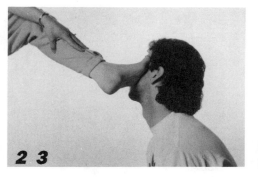

Ball of foot striking to the temple.

Natural Body
...Shin

The shin applies as a weapon much like the forearm—you can strike with a lot of power, and the length of the bone allows less accuracy than attacking with the foot. Depending on the position and situation, the shin may be used to strike the groin, face or neck.

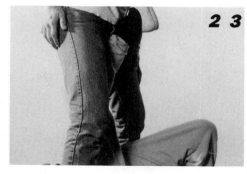

From the floor, crushing attacker's groin with shin.

Natural Body
...Foot

Toes and ball of foot slapping down across the nose and eyes.

Jabbing with toes to penetrate throat.

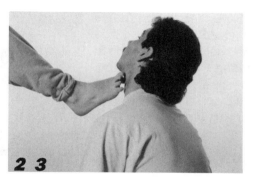

A head butt can break the assailant's nose.

Natural Body
...Head

Many potential victims of assault may find themselves in a situation where they are unable to move. It is at this time to remember to use your head—literally. The close range of a bear hug or other ways an attacker might grab place you in striking distance to butt with the forehead (soccer-style) or with the back of the head.

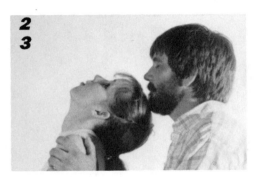

Attacking behind with head butt to jaw.

Natural Body
...Teeth

As a last effort to free yourself from an aggressive hold, you may resort to biting. Obviously, our teeth are designed to tear flesh and even break the bones of fingers if necessary.

Take a chunk out of the attacker's neck to stop his assault.

Miscellaneous

There are a multitude of products which are manufactured as actual weapons. They are designed for concealment as well as ease of use. Most of these items are easily purchased; a few are illegal in some states; nearly all require practice in order to develop effective use. In your practice, work to develop speed and accuracy with these products. If you fail to achieve your defense immediately, the weapon could be taken from you and used by an assailant.

The weapons discussed here are among the most common, most practical and most easily learned. They are no more complicated than other Implement Weapons and should be applied with the same timing and concentration. These weapons improve your chances of surprising an assailant due to their small size, intensity of effect, and their "double identity" as belts, key chains, jewelry and decorations.

Write to us for a list of manufacturers of the weapons in this chapter and hundreds of others not shown.

Miscellaneous
...Key chain knife

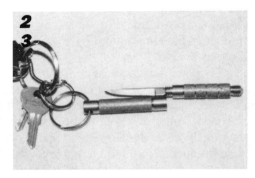

Quality knives range in size from the largest hunting knives to those small enough to carry in your pocket; some are even made specifically as key chains.

These are ideal Implement Weapons, as they can be opened and ready before you walk to or from your house, car, or office. They are concealed well enough to cause shock and confusion, sharp enough to cause severe injury, and small enough that they cannot be easily taken away.

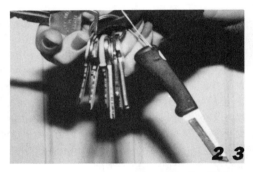

Key Chain Knives

Miscellaneous
...Mace®

Mace® is one of those products designed specifically for self defense. Its spray will temporarily blind and disorient the assailant, allowing you to escape or, if necessary, to perform a technique inflicting a higher degree of injury.

You can use your can of Mace® even if it becomes clogged or empty: attack with the can as with any other Implement Weapon.

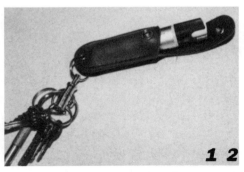

Key-chain sized Mace® spray.

Miscellaneous
...Cane & Stiletto

With criminals so commonly targeting the elderly as their victims, ladies might consider walking with a cane whether they need it or not. There are a number of options for using a cane as a weapon. The one that quickly comes to mind is the cliché little old lady beating the man in the head as she cries, "Masher!"

Because striking in this way can be easily blocked, other cane techniques should be rehearsed: for example, a straight jab with the tip; striking across to

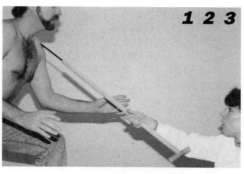

Cane with hidden stiletto blade.

the knees; or pulling the crooked end up into the groin. Canes with retracting stiletto blades are manufactured as weapons. With the press of a button revealing a needle-sharp blade, you can increase the effect of your defense from first- or second-degree injury to third degree.

Miscellaneous
...Lipstick knife

Another of the disguised weapons is the lipstick knife. A weapon such as this will give you the element of surprise, as it can be taken out discreetly, and is so small that the attacker will be confused by the cuts it inflicts. This is another item which can be carried in your purse, ready when you need it.

Lipstick Knife

Miscellaneous
...Belt knife

The belt knife lends itself to immediate reaction and surprise attack. It can also be taken out in advance of walking across a darkened parking lot or other dangerous environment. Its location on you could make a personal violation quite a surprise for the attacker.

Belt Knife hidden in buckle.

Miscellaneous
...Metal fan

The folding fan was a weapon which developed into a highly stylized art form in the Orient. Today you can see fan dancers gracefully repeating the movements created as fighting techniques. Then, the fans had sharp metal or wooden spikes on the tips of each rib. The points were often dipped in poison, making this combat the "dance of death."

Edges of metal fan used to cut attacker's neck.

Perhaps Scarlett O'Hara's fan will make a fashion comeback as women realize its utility in self defense. Good targets and methods include whipping open edges across the eyes or throat and poking with the folded fan.

Stabbing downward with end of folded fan.

Miscellaneous
...Key Chain Weapons

There are several key rings which are made to be weapons for self defense. One, the Kubotan, is a straight wooden or metal spike. It may be either flat or pointed on the end. This small weapon is easily concealed and may be used for gouging or poking.

Another weapon is called the spiked or Ninja key ring. This piece is larger than the Kubotan. Its spikes protrude from the hand through the knuckles and will cause a normal punch to penetrate the skin deeply. A third spike extends from the bottom of the fist.

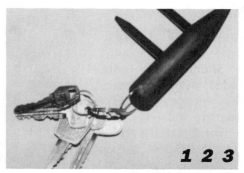

Spiked or "Ninja" Key Ring

Punch with spiked key ring to penetrate heart area.

Miscellaneous
...Stun gun

Electric shock devices on the market pack more punch than ever. The weapons release a charge that ranges from causing discomfort and confusion to temporarily disabling the attacker. Make sure to keep the stun gun charged!

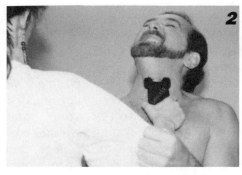

Stun Gun disables attacker.

Miscellaneous
...Shuriken

Shurikens are multi-bladed throwing "stars". They are heavy enough to penetrate the body when thrown forcefully and accurately—expect to spend hours practicing with a target. A possible use which would require less training would be to hold the weapon in your hand and use it to cut or stab an assailant. Shurikens would generally be available unsharpened as decorations, key chains, and even necklaces.

Shurikens come in a variety of shapes and sizes.

Miscellaneous
...Whistle

There are a number of electronic personal alarms on the market. These will emit a loud sound with the push of a button or the pull of a switch, signalling that an attack is in progress. The least expensive personal alarm, however, is a good, shrill whistle.

Most any potential attacker can be warded off by the loud, attention-getting sound. At close range, the noise is painfully deafening and confusing. Consider

Shrill whistle fends off attack.

placing a whistle on your key ring or carrying one in your purse. Keychain whistles are handed out on college campuses during orientation and "rape prevention week."

Summary

Think about it: Right now, if you are attacked, where is your weapon? Your awareness of Implement Weaponry should greatly increase with the study of this handbook. If you are genuinely concerned with being able to protect yourself, then make it a point, no matter where you are or what you are doing, to look around you and become more conscious of the items which may be utilized in defending yourself. You must be willing to fight back and protect yourself with whatever means possible. Each day in the United States, there are thousands of crimes of every imaginable sort committed against women. Men are repeatedly abusing their wives, the female workforce is being sexually harrassed, date and acquaintance rape is a common occurrance, robberies are committed on our streets in broad daylight, women are abducted from shopping mall parking lots, and the list goes on forever.

What will be your reaction if you are victimized? To submit to a crime committed against you may not be the best decision. The knowledge presented in this book should provide you with alternatives. If you were to suddenly find yourself in a situation from which you cannot escape, the use of an Implement Weapon could save you.

Attacks and physical violations may occur anywhere, anytime, by anyone. Don't let it happen to you. Take a stand. Say no. Resist.

Finally, to those women who are seriously interested in pursuing advanced levels of skill in self defense, it is recommended that you seek out a high quality martial arts program and train to black belt status.

Quiz Scoring:
"Are You a Target?"

1. A = 1   B = 0   C = 2
2. Score 1 Point for YES answers to B or D.
   Score 1 Point for NO answers to A, C, or E.
3. A = 0   B = 1   C = 2
4. Score 1 Point each.
5. Score 1 Point for answer 2. to situation A or B.
   Score 1 Point for answer 1. to situation C.
6. Score 1 Point for each YES answer.
7. A, B, or C = 1   D or E = 0
8. If your total was 0-5, score 3 Points. For 6-10 steps taken, score 2 Points.
   If you counted 11-15, score 1 Point. For 16-20, add no Points, and if you
   observe 21 or more safety precautions, subtract 1 Point from your score.
9. Score 1 Point if you AGREE with statement A or B.
   Score 1 Point if you DISAGREE with statement C, D, or E.
10. A = 0   B = 2   C = 2
11. A = 0   B = 1   C = 1
    D = 2   E = 3
12. A = 0   B = 2   C = 1
13. Score 1 Point for YES.
14. Score 1 Point for NO.

This is one quiz on which you would want to score a "0".
Chances are that you did not. However, if your points total fewer
than 11, you have made a good start on protecting yourself from
being targeted for crime. Study and rehearse the techniques in this
book to be ready should an attack occur.

If your score falls in the narrow range from 11 to 18, you
probably tend to carry yourself with good confidence but perhaps
not enough attention to the very real statistics on crime against
women.

If you are among those to score higher than 18, you may be
flirting with disaster. The latest crime reports have estimated that a
woman's odds of being assaulted have risen to 1 in 3. To decrease
your chances of being targeted for crime, pay particular attention to
the chapter, *Be in Control*, which outlines crime-prevention measures. Study this book thoroughly and use it to establish new safety
habits and improve your "S.Q." (safety quotient). The very fact that
you are reading this book already demonstrates your concern.

Personal Safety Profile
Part I...Crime and Attack Prevention

The chapter, *Be in Control* (page 3), lists more than 25 steps you can take to prevent a crime happening to you. Review the chapter and count how many of those steps you regularly perform. Work on memorizing these precautions and developing safe habits. You will become more aware of your safety (and of potential dangers) by concentrating each week on one or two new ways of protecting yourself.

In addition to taking specific steps to prevent crime, a woman must prepare herself for the possibility of being targeted as a victim. The chapter, *If you are a Victim*, outlines a series of reactions to follow when confronted by an attacker. Memorize the six steps, review them periodically, and try to picture yourself going through the process.

Personal Safety Profile
Part II...Improving Your "S.Q."
(Safety Quotient)

Part II of your Personal Saftey Profile involves your response to the results of Part I, "Are You a Target?" Each "safe" answer added no points to your score. Review your own answers to the questions. For each answer that added to your score, ask yourself if the answer can be changed and if so, how you can change it to improve your Personal Safety score.

Example for Question #1:

If your style of dress contributes to your risk as a target, what can you do to change it? Idea 1—Today's fashions are quite revealing. Invest in a full-length coat to wear between your car and your destination. Idea 2—High heels inhibit balance and mobility. Make a habit to wear sturdy walking or running shoes on your way to and from the office.

Example for Question #2:

If shyness and timidity make you vulnerable, enroll in a martial arts or assertiveness training course to build self-confidence. You can also challenge and overcome this tendency to be timid through sheer determination and practice, if you have the will to go it alone.

Some of your "unsafe" responses to this quiz you may be unwilling or unable to change, such as your physical characteristics or your work schedule. These you should compensate for in other areas, such as observing all preventive measures, and by your study of Implement Weaponry.

Personal Safety Profile
Part III...Implement Weaponry Quiz

Make a list of Implement Weapons available to you at this very moment. After studying this book you should be able to come up with quite a few. Hint: this book is one. Don't worry if some of the weapons on your list are not included in these pages—it shows that you truly have learned that...

...ANYTHING IS A WEAPON!

About the Author

Rodney R. Rice was born in Radford, Virginia in 1955. He was raised on a farm in the Shenandoah Valley and later moved to Northern Virginia, completing his education. As an adult, he made his career in the martial arts, and after twenty years training and experience achieved Master Instructor. Rice is the owner of two of the nation's largest martial arts schools in Fredericksburg and Warrenton, Virginia, consisting of hundreds of students. He is well known for his talents and dedication as a teacher and produces scores of black belts each year. In 1990, he founded the Black Belt College of America, a national organization which is committed to certifying black belts and instructors.

Rice comments, "The true quality of the artist is his ability to be expressive and creative." Just as no two painters paint alike or no two musicians compose alike, it is the same in the world of martial artists. When they compete in the ring or perform on the stage, the people can detect the beauty and poise of their art. The desire for perfection will push a person beyond their normal capabilities. A true artist strives to satisfy the eye of the audience and strives to meet their desire.

Rice's motivation for creating *101 Weapons for Women: Implement Weaponry* comes from a sincere desire to give women the knowledge of what they really need to do to stop an attacker. Women are asking, "What can I do to prevent a crime from being committed against me?" This has always been a burden to Rice, as self defense is his business. The production of this book is his contribution to fighting the crimes against women.

Rodney R. Rice